MARGARET SINCLAIR

Nihil Obstat

MGR. HENRICUS FORBES,

Censor Deputatus.

Imprimatur

✠MGR. JOANNES CANON RITCHIE,

Vic. Gen.

GLASGUAE,

14ᵃ *Octobris*, 1927.

Frontispiece

Blackfriars Street, showing the house where
Margaret Sinclair lived, marked X

MARGARET SINCLAIR

IN RELIGION

SISTER MARY FRANCIS
OF THE FIVE WOUNDS

Extern Sister of the Poor Clare Colettines

BY

F. A. FORBES

WITH A PREFACE BY HIS GRACE THE ARCHBISHOP OF GLASGOW

"I know, my God, that Thou lovest simplicity."

PARAL. 29, 17.

LONDON: SANDS & CO.
15 KING STREET, COVENT GARDEN, W.C.,
AND AT EDINBURGH AND GLASGOW

First Edition *1927*
Second Edition *1928*

PRINTED IN GREAT BRITAIN BY
NORTHUMBERLAND PRESS LIMITED, NEWCASTLE-UPON-TYNE

To

the Friends of God who have helped me
by prayer, labour, courtesy, encouragement
and advice, and without whom this book
could never have been written.

FOREWORD

THE following pages are the record of a
lowly, unpretending life, the short, uneventful
—as the world goes—life of a Scottish girl,
Margaret Sinclair, who was born, grew up
and lived in circumstances practically identical
with those in which the vast majority of girls
and boys are born, grow up and live to-day.
We are all familiar with those circumstances
and surroundings, and whether we look at
them from within or from without, we are
aware that in many ways they are not such
as human beings would choose, had they
unrestricted freedom in the matter.

Too often there is in our homes—when
there is a home—the constant uncertainty of
even limited material provision for the present
and the future, an uncertainty branching off
into countless crops of worries and anxieties.

Too often, outside the home there is much that is coarsening, deadening or worse, in full play on the unshielded avenues to the heart and soul of plastic childhood and ardent youth. Can girls and boys, can young men and women in such an environment keep clear and bright the remembrance of their high destiny? Can they break the iron tyranny of circumstances, weather in triumph their stormy buffetings and shape their lives faithfully to God's plans? Or must beauty of life, perfection of virtue, become with each day that passes something more and more remote, an intangible dream at best, an impossibility?

I find in the life of Margaret Sinclair a most decided answer to those questions. The answer is—with God's help, beauty of life and perfection of virtue are within the reach of all. Further, the life of Margaret Sinclair is a proof that in the essential business of life and in the matter of true happiness circumstances and surroundings are not the decisive factor. In her life there is forcibly brought out once more, and on the familiar stage of

present-day Scotland, the truth that what
really counts is to face with simplicity the
issues before one, whatever be one's condition, to place one's joy in doing to the
best of one's power the task each day brings,
to remember constantly that in the journey
through life we are in the keeping of wiser
counsels than human intelligence can devise.

I find a singular beauty in the life of
Margaret Sinclair—this frail modern Scottish
girl—in all its settings. I notice that she was
far from being naturally dead to the ordinary
attractions of life; that she was sensitive and
affectionate; liked nice things and felt being
often without them. I also see with what
winsomeness she set herself to rule herself, to
avoid impatience, sourness, gloom, to practise
the real courtesies of life in the thousand
details of her daily routine. Above all, I
observe how she made Our Lord in the
Blessed Sacrament the centre and the inspiration of her life. What wonder, then, if she
learnt from Him in most ample measure that
delicacy and refinement which gave fragrance
to virtue, that thoughtfulness and con-

siderateness which she was perceived by all
to possess? What wonder if her life is
singularly beautiful? For beauty, on every
plane, in all its embodiments, is God mirrored
in His Creation.

May the example of her life be an inspiration to all, but especially to the thousands of
young men and women who, whatever be their
position in life, find themselves harassed,
perplexed, unhappy.

✠ D. MACKINTOSH,
Archbishop of Glasgow.

Bearsden,
30th September, 1927.

CONTENTS

LIST OF ILLUSTRATIONS

XV

CHAPTER I

INTRODUCTORY

" The soul perfected by humility says : ' My Lord,
behold Thy handmaid, be it done unto me according to
Thy word, and not according to what I want with my
senses.' So it sheds the fragrance of patience around the
Creator and its fellow-creature and itself. It has peace
and quiet in its mind, and it has found peace in warfare,
because it has driven far from it its self-will founded in
pride, and has conceived divine grace in its soul. And
it bears in its breast Christ crucified, and seeks to know
naught but Christ crucified; and its bed is the Cross of
Christ crucified. There it annuls its own will, and
becomes humble and obedient."—St. CATHERINE OF SIENA.

Two poor working-girls were overheard not
long ago discussing the question of sanctity.
One spoke enthusiastically of St. Theresa of
Lisieux. "Yes," said the other, after a
moment's reflection, "the Little Flower was
all very well, but then, you see, she was

guarded and kept from evil all her life.   Now
Margaret Sinclair grew up in the midst of it,
just like ourselves."

"Just like ourselves"—that is perhaps the
secret of the wonderful appeal of the life-story
of Margaret Sinclair to those who, amid the
same trials and temptations, are living the
same life as she did.   Across the sordid background of the worker in the world of to-day
flits the radiant figure of a little Edinburgh
working-girl—an inspiration and a joy.

Among the people—of all ranks in life, and
often miles asunder—who have recorded their
impressions of Margaret Sinclair, the word
"radiant" is the one which occurs most often.
Hers was a radiant spirit, and it communi-
cated — and still communicates — itself to
others.   "I cannot tell you how my girls love
her," wrote a mother quite lately; "they say
it[1] has just made life worth living."   "The
girls in this factory," writes another, "try

---

[1] The little booklet *Margaret Sinclair,* by Father Agius,
S.J., published by Sands & Co.

to imitate Margaret Sinclair by daily Communion. The 'Life' has made a wonderful change in this place. We are all so happy."

From her childhood Margaret sowed happiness wherever she went, and she does so still. Her sister tells us that when, as a child on the school playground, she noticed that any of the other children were in trouble or out of sorts, she would go to them, and would not leave them " till they were as cheerful as she was." She worked more by example than by words, for she was a true Scot in her reserve about herself and everything that concerned her. " She never spoke directly of religious things," writes a friend of her girlhood. " She made me think more of God; I wanted to go to Mass and to Holy Communion every morning, just to be like her, though she did not ask this of me."

" She liked to be a little saint without anyone knowing it," says her sister; yet Margaret was encouragingly human. She liked pretty clothes, and made them for herself with deft

fingers. She liked dancing—especially with her father, " because he could not dance very well and she used to have great fun trying to teach him." She was naturally quick tempered, and her happy serenity of spirit was not maintained without a struggle. She once confessed to her sister that the little prayer, " Jesus, meek and humble of heart, make my heart like to Thine," was often the only thing that kept her from losing her temper completely. She would sometimes go out of the room rather suddenly and come in again after a few moments, her own smiling self again. " It is the best way for me," she said to the same sister, " for if I did not, I might say something I would be sorry for afterwards." If a family disagreement seemed impending, Margaret would make some quaint remark that made everyone burst out laughing; as a child, she would do the same when sharp words were flying among her young companions. " She would change everything into sunshine."

There were other things about Margaret that may well uplift our courage and strengthen our faith. Her whole life was an answered prayer. If she was "so wise," it was because she prayed to the Holy Ghost for wisdom. If she conquered temptation, it was because she knew the power of the Holy Name of Jesus, and used it to the full. If she was pure, it was because she kept herself, by daily Communion, in close touch with the God of all purity. If her patience in suffering was a marvel to all who knew her, it was because she had prayed, her whole life long, that God's Holy Will might be done in her. She took the little things of life and worked her way to sanctity through them.

Margaret Sinclair was born and brought up amidst the sordid surroundings of an Edinburgh slum, while St. Theresa of the Child Jesus was shielded from every form of evil— yet they were certainly soul-sisters. The same fragrance of childlike simplicity clings about them both, the same burning love of God

consumed them, the same forgetfulness of self and zeal for souls characterized them. " She was another Little Flower," wrote one who knew her of Margaret, and a priest who saw her during her last illness at Warley, spoke of her as " that little white violet, the Poor Clare nun." Another priest wrote asking for her prayers—for " the simple, charming, spiritual beauty of her face and soul haunts the memory."

A radiant spirit indeed. " No picture," says a nun in a convent where Margaret made a retreat shortly before she entered the Poor Clares, " can reproduce her fair, pale face with its angelic expression. It was holiness at its mightiest that this humble, simple child was aiming at; one felt the depths beyond fathoming of the childlike earnestness, the single-mindedness and purity which wins the Kingdom of Heaven even in this world."

As the sweet-faced child " who never sulked or resented correction"; as the " unaffected, simple working-girl, who sanctified herself and

others by living her ordinary daily life perfectly, doing her duty conscientiously for men
and giving God His due "; as the extern Sister
of the Poor Clares who lay in the Sanatorium
at Warley gasping out her life with such a
radiant face that the awed watchers asked her
if she were smiling at the angels—she was the
same Margaret—a little sunbeam of God sent
to give joy in a dingy world.

It belongs to Holy Church alone to pro-
nounce on the sanctity of her children, but,
day by day, from many different quarters,
comes the account of wonderful graces,
conversions and cures, obtained through
Margaret's intercession. They are being
investigated by the Committee appointed for
that purpose, and will not be related here.
One very small incident alone I will mention,
and that because, in the first place, it is so
delightfully like a fairy tale, and in the second
—it is so like Margaret. I tell it as it was
told to me :

Two wee children of Edinburgh, poor as

was Margaret herself in the days of her childhood, watched the aeroplanes which went up
during the summer months for a short circular
flight.   They longed with all their little souls
to be in one, but a ticket cost five shillings.
Five shillings seemed a fortune to them, and
quite unattainable, and, even if they had had
such a sum and spent it in going up in an
aeroplane, their mother would certainly have
whipped them.

One day they had a bright idea. " Let us
ask Margaret Sinclair to pray for us, d'ye
mind how good she was to the wee ones,
giving them a swing? "   They set off to the
church, knelt down, and said their three Hail
Mary's, and " Margaret Sinclair, pray for us."
As they came out they met one of the teachers,
whom they knew.   "Miss," they pleaded,
" wad ye gie us threepence to get into the
aerodrome? "   She gave them threepence
each, and they went off happily.

But, even inside the aerodrome, they were
no nearer to the required five shillings—or

rather—since there were two of them—ten! There they stood, their wee hearts away up in the aeroplane and their bodies, alas, on the ground.

Suddenly a gentleman who was passing near them stopped. " Would you like to go up in the aeroplane? " he asked.

Would they like to go up?—there was no doubt about that! He produced from his pocket two tickets. " I bought these for my two children," he said, " and they are crying, and saying they will not go. Here you are! " He put them into their eager hands and went away.

Margaret had played up—and the bairnies went up in the aeroplane.

CHAPTER II

CHILDHOOD

" Here is Thy footstool and there rest Thy feet, where live the poorest and lowliest and lost.

" O Master Poet, I have sat down at Thy feet. Only let me make my life simple and straight, like a flute of reed for Thee to fill with music."—R.T.

MARGARET SINCLAIR was born in Edinburgh on the 29th of March, 1900. Her father, Andrew Sinclair, worked as a scavenger under the City Corporation; her mother, Elizabeth Kelly, was a native of Dundee. Andrew Sinclair was not a Catholic, but Elizabeth converted him, and he was received into the Church several months before their marriage.

Mrs. Sinclair was a good Catholic mother. When Margaret lay dying in the Sanatorium of the Sisters of Charity at Warley, she spoke

of how her mother, when she was bathing the little ones, would reverently make the sign of the Cross over their five senses, saying : " May you never offend Him." " How happy we are to have such a good father and mother," she used constantly to say to her sister, as they grew up together.

Margaret, the second daughter and the third child of her parents, was born at a house in Middle Arthur Place, but the family soon moved to Blackfriars Street, in the parish of St. Patrick's.

Blackfriars Wynd, as this street was called until quite recently, derived its name from the old Monastery of the Black Friars or Dominicans, which stood, in pre-Reformation days, on the site of the old infirmary. Though now it ranks among the slums of Edinburgh, four hundred years ago it was one of the most aristocratic quarters of the city, and is full of historic interest. On the eastern side of the street stood the palace of Archbishop James Beaton, later occupied by his nephew the

Cardinal, who entertained James V more than once within its walls. The Regent Morton—of unsavoury memory—had a house there, which is still to be seen, and the Wynd is further noted as the rallying point in the famous faction fight between Arran and Angus, known as " Cleanse the Causey."

More remarkable still, perhaps, is the fact that in Blackfriars Wynd, in olden times, stood the town house of " the lordly line of high St. Clair," Earls of Orkney and Rosslyn, a family which, we are told, reached the highest pinnacle of its splendour in the person of Earl William. His lady-wife was wont to be attended by " seventy-five gentlewomen, of whom fifty-three were daughters of noblemen, all clothed in velvets and silks, with chains of gold." When this great lady rode abroad—and she must have found the narrow Wynd rather strait for her retinue—" two hundred belted knights " escorted her, and when she returned home, after dark, " eighty pages, all of noble birth," accompanied her with torches

St. Patrick's Church, where Margaret Sinclair was baptised and made her first Communion.

Photo, Fairer.

to light her on her way. Her ladyship would have been considerably astonished to hear that, many centuries later, when the neighbourhood had fallen from its high repute, the humble daughter of a city scavenger would lend a higher lustre to the name of Sinclair than it had ever known in the days of its greatest glory. " For the noble chivalry of the heart may belong to him who walks barefoot or in rags, whereas he who is without it, though richly clothed, is ignoble."[1]

Margaret, says her mother, was always " a wise and sensible child," unselfish and thoughtful for others : " always tryin' to dae something for ye, from her youngest day." " I wish I was a big girl, Mother," she said one day when only three years old, " to be able to work and help you." There was indeed plenty to be done in the little household, for the bairnies came in rather quick succession, and there were already five when Margaret spoke.

When she was about five years old, Margaret

[1] Kenelm Digby, *The Broad Stone of Honour.*

began to go with her sister Bella, two years her senior, to the Catholic school of St. Anne's, in charge of the Sisters of Mercy. Andrew, nearly two years younger, was the next to join the school party. He adored Margaret, and Bella complained that they could never get away from him for a minute. " Poor wee soul," Margaret would answer compassionately, " he has no little boys to play with—let him come."

Margaret, though the younger, soon outstripped her sister at school. While the two were in the same class she would help Bella with her lessons. " She was so good to me, so thoughtful and charitable," says the elder sister, " that I am not afraid to say that in the whole school there was not another like her."

Her schoolfellows speak of her as " jolly and bright, always laughing and ready for fun. She used to talk of games and swimming, and about going to Confession and Communion." " She had a good word for everybody," says another. " She never tried to get her own way

in any of the games," says her sister, "and if she was playing with anything and anyone else wanted it, she gave it up at once." This seems to have been characteristic of her—at home as well as at school.

Margaret's teachers have nothing special to say of her, excepting that she was a quiet, docile child, who never resented correction and who gave no trouble—" a child who tried to serve God and practise her religion." She worked hard and tried to get on. One who taught her remembers her as a " pale-faced, large-eyed little mouse, with a sweet expression."

Her pale face was perhaps due to the fact that those were lean days in the Sinclair family. By this time there were six children to clothe and feed, and the eldest boy was not yet fourteen. It was hard, with the strictest economy, to make both ends meet, and it became harder still when the breadwinner of the family fell ill and was three months in the infirmary. One day Margaret, going bare-

foot to Mass after a scanty breakfast, fainted in the church. "The child is not properly clothed or fed," said the person who attended to her.

Then Mrs. Sinclair herself had a severe illness, and she kept the ten-year-old Margaret at home to help her, rather than her elder sister. "She was so wise," says her mother, "and so helpful. And she was so silent; she never spoke outside of what she had seen or done at home." "Mother, don't say '*will* ye do this,'" she used to say, "say '*do it*.'" When she was even younger she would urge her mother: "Mother, ye shouldna say '*will* ye?'"

At the age of ten Margaret made her first Communion. She was prepared, with the other children of St. Patrick's, by Father George Lennett, now Bishop of Aberdeen. Here again, the silent little girl kept her secrets to herself, and no one remembers anything striking about her. She would often say later, says her brother Andrew, that it had

Margaret Sinclair as a Child.

been the happiest day of her life, but she gave no further details. Her elder sister, Isabella, made her first Communion with her, and the two were confirmed together by Archbishop Smith on the same day. "Oh, she *was* so happy that day," says her sister.

By this time the smallest girl, Lizzie, was going to school with the others. She was a delicate little thing and—according to her own description—"impudent." "Bella wouldn't be bothered with me." So it was Margaret who shouldered the responsibility. She was a tender little mother to the wee sister; getting her up in the morning, washing and dressing her, and saving up her halfpennies—they were very few—to buy her a bright hair-ribbon. When the children came out for recreation, she would wait for Lizzie, who was with the little ones, and devote all her playtime to her, though she loved play and was one of the best among those of her own age at the school games. On cold days she would ask leave to

c

take the little sister into one of the class-rooms,
or make her run to warm herself. When it
was very cold and the child was shivering, she
would take her on her knee and tuck the two
little cold hands inside her own pinafore
against her warm heart. "I used to wonder,"
says Lizzie, "at the heat that came from
Margaret's pinny."

Even when she grew older, Margaret still
continued to mother her little sister. "She
was always reminding me to look cheerful,"
says Lizzie, "no matter how gloomy I felt,
for she said a cheerful face makes others
happy. She taught me all my home lessons,
even the sums of the higher classes. One of
the teachers remarked to me on this the first
day I was in her class, and asked me who had
helped me. She told the others that she
wished they had elder sisters who would take
the same trouble with them and help them in
the same way."

"She was like a second mother to me; her
gentle ways made me love her. I always

looked upon her as older than Bella, for she was less impulsive and seemed more experienced in her ways. She used to notice the Sisters saying their rosary in the playground, and often spoke to me of the beauty of a nun's life of prayer."

When it was time for Lizzie to make her first Communion, as the family finances did not admit of a new white dress for her, Margaret promptly suggested that she should make down her own to fit her, and did it so successfully—for even as a child she had clever fingers — that the little girl was delighted.

"We used to play in a yard where there were swings," says Bella. It was the playground of St. Anne's school, which runs along behind the back windows of the houses in Blackfriars Street. When the little Sinclairs were enjoying themselves on the swings, other children who had none, would stand looking at them with wistful eyes. Margaret was always the first to notice them. "Let us give them all

twenty each on our swing," she would say,
" and make them happy."

Bella would see them sometimes talking
together and pointing at Margaret. " D'ye
see that girl? " they would say, " she *is* such
a nice girl; she gave us swings."

Margaret had her own ideas on the subject
of familiarity, and avoided children who were
rough and ill-mannered. She was coming
back one day from doing a message, and had
just reached the house door, when a little boy
of about her own age, who was playing in the
street, caught her by the arm, saying : " Oh,
my little darling." Margaret went quickly
into the house, deposited her parcel on the
table, and as quickly went out again. A few
moments later she returned—rather flushed
and breathless. " What is the matter? " asked
her mother. " He won't say that to me
again," said Margaret, with decision, " for I
have given him a good lesson." She was
quite serious, but when everyone began to
laugh, she laughed with them. Her father

kept it up against her as a joke. "But I was quite right," Margaret would answer, smiling.

"She would save up her halfpennies—for we seldom got a whole penny," says Bella, "to buy a little Christmas present for Father and Mother. She usually got it at the penny bazaar, and Father and Mother used to be more than delighted, little though it was. When we had a mission, and we children went to the chapel after school, she would tell them all about it when she got home—the nice sermon, and the nice little stories that the Father who was giving the mission had told us, and how we had had Benediction after-wards—which she loved.

"When it came round to Lent or Christmas she used to have a little piece of paper on which she would make a cross for every Hail Mary she said. She would say a thousand, or even ten thousand, to give the Baby Jesus a little present. As we got up a long time before we went to school, she used to say quite

a lot, and she was so happy when she found she had said so many.

"Sometimes she would say: 'Let us see who can keep silence the longest' so that we could get more said. When she was tempted to laugh during her prayers, she told me that she would picture to herself our Divine Lord with His Head crowned with thorns, and it always made her grave.

"She wanted to go to all the churches at Christmas, to see where the Baby Jesus was the best arranged, and she loved to burn candles there. But she had not the pennies when we were at school, though when she left, Mother used to give her two or three. She used to make many little sacrifices for Lent and Christmas, such as taking her tea without sugar and her bread without butter, or remaining silent when anyone contradicted her. She was very charitable to the poor blind people, and those who used to sing in the street. When they were young people she used to say: 'I am sure they would work if they could,

St. Anne's School and Playground.

but perhaps they can't get work. Anyhow, if you give for the love of God, it is all right.'

"She would hurry home from school to help Mother," says Bella, "and Mother liked to have her very much to lend a hand with the housework." On one evening during the week Mrs. Sinclair went to a mothers' sewing party in the Canongate, managed by the Helpers of the Holy Souls, who had charge of the mothers' meetings of St. Patrick's. "Then we would all set to work to give her a surprise when she came home. ' I shall tidy up the fireplace, or wash the floor,' Margaret would say, and John would help us. Margaret and I used to laugh many times afterwards at the remembrance of those evenings. John, with an old apron on, helping to clean, though Andrew made a better attempt at cleaning than John. John would take his turn of minding the baby, and when the baby cried John nearly cried too—for he was very fond of reading, and when baby cried he could

not get on with his story. And, when it was raining, and Mother stayed in the house, Andrew would get hold of her long black skirt and a white towel, covering his forehead and hanging down behind, and then he would act as a nun. The rest of us used to be very pleased with him, for we thought he made a very nice nun. At other times he would act as a priest and say Mass and give us all blessings, but not often, as Mother thought it was not right to amuse ourselves like that. But she did not mind about the nun —unless he did something she did not approve of."

It was a happy family party, in spite of poverty. "Father and Mother were just like a big brother and sister to us," says Bella. "Margaret loved very much when the Forty Hours' Adoration came round, for Father would take us all to the chapels we did not know the way to, such as Leith, Portobello, Dalkeith, Slateford, etc. He always gave us time to say the five decades of the rosary. And

Blackfriars Street, from the High Street.

he always got us a good place, where we could see the whole altar. Margaret would kneel there, so still. She never turned round to see who was behind her, and when she got home she would say : ' I wish it was not so far away, so that I could go by myself.' "

In after years their mother used to tell them how their father, who had to go out to his work at half-past five, had to wait, fasting, when he was going to Holy Communion, until half-past seven, when the Mass began. One or two other Catholics, scavengers like himself, thought no harm in taking a quiet smoke in their carts while they were waiting, but he would never do it, thinking it more reverent to make the sacrifice for his Lord and Master.

"Father was so good," says Bella. " He gave all his money to Mother and only kept a little for himself, for tobacco. There are not many fathers who would do that. Mother would never dress herself up and leave us out, like some mothers who lived near us. If

Father had saved up a little money—for he was very obliging and often got tips—he would say to her : ' I am sure you could put that to some good use ; it is no good harbouring it up.' Then Mother would be delighted. ' I shall get something for the children with it,' she would say. ' For goodness sake get something for yourself and leave the children alone,' he would answer. She seldom got anything for herself, and when she did it was always black—till Margaret and I grew up, and then we made her get something with a little colour. Margaret would often say to me : ' The Sinclairs are all richer than we are, but we have the riches of all riches and the best happiness of all—for we are Catholics and have such a good father and mother.' "

Someone who took an interest in the family, hearing that the youngest boy was ill, went one Sunday morning, at about twelve o'clock, to make inquiries. He was immensely struck with the air of refinement and the happy family spirit which prevailed in the living-room

where they were all together, the two elder
girls preparing the dinner. Mrs. Sinclair was
grateful for the kind thought that had prompted
the visit, and the visitor sat down and had a
long talk with her. She did not like the dis-
trict, she said, and would prefer to go to better
surroundings, but times were very bad and
they could not afford it. It was necessary,
now that the girls were growing up, that they
should have a room to themselves, though the
keeping up of a three-roomed house was almost
more than they could manage. Her extreme
solicitude about this—not too usual in that
locality—impressed him much. It happened
that on his way to see them he had met a
friend who had given him five pounds, asking
him to bestow it where it was deserved—and
needed. " Would a pound be of any use to
you? " he asked Mrs. Sinclair, and was much
touched by her gratitude. He saw the two
elder girls with their mother, later, at a social
evening at St. Patrick's, and was once more
struck by their gentleness and refinement.

" Margaret," says her sister, " was always very smart at school; she liked to be clean and tidy." Later on, she tells us that Margaret liked pretty clothes, and was very handy at making them, both for herself and for the little ones. Before she left school she went for a short time, after school hours, to do messages at a fancy-work shop in the town, but when the " messages " developed into scrubbing down stairs and passages, the child came home so tired at night that her mother put a stop to it. When the two elder girls were both at work things became a little easier, and the pinch of poverty was less acutely felt.

The two sisters, while still at school, used to go several times a week to night classes for sewing, cooking and dressmaking. Margaret won certificates for attendance and diligence which enabled her to attend the High School at Atholl Crescent, which she greatly appreciated. She also won certificates for running and swimming, for she was very good at all sports and games.

St. Anne's School, showing part of a 15th Century House,
included in the building.

When she was in the Supplementary Class, Margaret first began to go to daily Mass and Communion, a practice which she kept up later.

CHAPTER III

AT WORK

" Love is an infinite compassion for the sorrows of others; happiness is a great love and much serving; and goodness is to take the little things of life and walk truly among them."—O.S.

When Margaret left school she took up french-polishing as an apprentice at the Waverley Cabinet Works. She was the only apprentice in the place, and the man in charge used often to slip out, leaving her his work to do as well as her own during his absence. Although this laid a heavy burden on her, it proved useful in the end, for it brought her practice and experience. When, owing to the war and the consequent slackness of business, the firm was obliged to close down, her employer gave

46

Margaret a recommendation to the Scottish Furniture Company as an excellent worker and a very good character. She was a tall girl for her age, and the last friendly hint of this first employer was to put up her hair. " It will make you look older, and you will get better pay," he said.

One little incident of this first apprenticeship is worth relating. Hidden away among some rubbish in the workshop Margaret found one day a beautiful picture of Our Lady. She dusted it and hung it up in the corner where she worked. Every day when she came back to her work, she found it had been taken down and hidden away again, and every day she brought it out, dusted it again, and—not without, we may be sure, a devout salutation to God's Mother—hung it up again. The silent duel continued until she left the place.

The story of Margaret's first whist-drive was long a joke in the Sinclair family. Mr. X, the visitor who has been already mentioned,

called one afternoon bringing tickets for the two girls for a whist-drive at St. Patrick's. Mrs. Sinclair, though grateful for the kind thought, was rather uneasy.   It was winter time, and she was doubtful of the wisdom of going for a drive on a cold, dark night.   However, she did not want to damp the girls' enjoyment or to deprive them of a pleasure, and merely told them, when they came in from work, that Mr. X had kindly brought them tickets for a whist-drive at St. Patrick's, and that they were to be sure to put on their warmest coats.

The girls took their tea, wrapped themselves up, and ran off.   Mrs. Sinclair, still uneasy, went with them to the door.   "Thank God there is a bright moon," she said.

It was not long, however, before the girls came running back, laughing heartily.   "It's a party, Mother," they cried, "they are all sitting at tables."   With great relief she helped them into their best blouses and saw them off again—this time without apprehen-

Margaret Sinclair at fifteen.

sions. Margaret, although she had never
played whist in her life, won a prize of five
shillings.

"She was very fond of dancing," says her
sister, "but when we went to a dance it was
nearly always connected with St. Patrick's, the
Sacred Heart or the Cathedral. Andrew and
Margaret were very good at it. Mother would
take us up for the old-fashioned dances, such
as a waltz or sets, and Andrew would give us a
chance of the later ones. When Andrew,
Margaret and I went without Mother, if
Margaret was up Andrew would take me,
and if I was up he would take Margaret, and
that was the way he passed his night, unless
Margaret told him to take up some girl friend
of hers. We always came home with him.
Margaret was very fond of him, for he was very
much her style."

Their girl friends used often to laugh at the
inseparableness of the Sinclair family. "If
you see one, you are sure to see the other, and
if one of you is alone, Andrew or your mother

are always with you." Margaret would laugh and say: "It is just habit." Even their mother would sometimes declare that one could not go the length of the street without the other. When the girls were alone together, says Bella, Margaret would speak with great joy of the happy union among them. "Look at that big family," she would say, "how happy they might be if they were united like us, but they have each their own little ways. They would hardly believe that we have such fun in our own little circle, instead of always looking for new friends and seldom being contented."

She would always say her rosary when she came home from a dance, though sometimes she was very tired. "I enjoyed myself very well," she would say, "and I must give God his share. Look at us dancing there and enjoying ourselves, and how many Religious Orders were up, praying for us, and how many souls God has called home during that time."

At night, when Margaret came home from her work, she would always, when passing the church, go in for a little visit to the Blessed Sacrament. Sometimes she stayed too long, and her mother, who did not like the girls to be out late, would scold her. Her friends would often say to her: "Why do you have to be home so early? I would not stand it." "Home is the best place," Margaret would answer, with her quiet smile.

"I don't know how she learned to know all the lives of the Saints," says Bella, "but she used to tell me such a lot about them when we were by ourselves. I know she was fond of buying the little books at the Sacred Heart, Lauriston[1]. Sometimes she would read them at her work and advise me to read those that she liked best. But I liked it better when she used to tell me the stories while we were washing up. I sometimes said that if she

[1] The church of the Jesuit Fathers in Edinburgh. She took the books from the C.T.S. stand at the end of the church.

would read me the story, I would do the washing-up.   Then she would laugh and say: 'It is a sin, I think, for me to encourage you; it is very simple and you would do better to read it for yourself.'   Then, when we were alone in the bedroom, I would go on asking her over and over again, and at last she would begin to read to me.   'Do you understand?' she would ask me when the words were rather long, and, if I did not, she would explain it to me—but there was never any pride about her when she was explaining.   I often wondered if I would have been as full of charity if I had been in her place, for not many younger sisters are as charitable as Margaret was to me."

These nocturnal readings were not so acceptable to the girls' father, who had to get up very early in the morning to go to his work.   He would often knock through the wall and tell them to go to sleep.   Margaret would sometimes ask him to call her when he got up, so that she might make his tea and help her

mother a little before she went to the church,
but sometimes she would be so tired that she
stayed in bed till it was time to get up for Mass.
Then her father would tease her: "What were
you doing this morning that you had to get up
so early?" he would ask in the evening.
Margaret would laugh. "I did not get up,"
she would say; "I will to-morrow, if God
spares me."

If the two girls had been out at their night
classes or at a Sunday evening Benediction,
and did not come in until after the family
rosary had been said, Margaret would insist
on saying it before going to bed. Then she
would take a big prayer-book of her father's,
of which she was very fond, and say: "What
shall we ask for to-night?" "There was one
prayer," says her sister, "asking for our
purgatory on earth, which she would never say.
I asked her why one night. 'I am afraid God
might make me a burden to Father and Mother,'
she said, 'otherwise I should love to have my
purgatory on earth. But I know that they

would work themselves to death to make me well again, and I should not like that.'" The prayers finished, she would do a little sewing, and then begin to pray again before she went to bed. Neighbours whose windows overlooked that of the girls' bedroom, have said how edified they often were at the sight of the two sisters with their prayer-book, reading and praying together in the evening when their work was done.

None of the Sinclairs had the pen of a ready writer. When the father and elder brother were away at the war, the family correspondence, as usual, fell to Margaret. Ideas would not always flow, and the writing day, when it came round, was occasionally something of a penance. One evening when Margaret, pen in hand, was busy at the table, her mother turned round suddenly, just in time to see her cutting off a good strip from the end of the sheet of paper. "So that's the way you write to John!" she said, "now I have caught you." Margaret was much abashed. "You turned too quickly,"

Margaret Sinclair at Sixteen.

she said, "I have often done it before." Then, heroically, "I will begin again." Then, "Shall I tell John what I have done?" "She was always so simple," says her mother.

Punctuation was not Margaret's strong point, and a postcard written to her father when he was away, was long kept up against her. "God keep you from your loving wife," it ran. When her father came home he produced it from his pocket and presented it to her. "Will ye read that, ma damsel," he said. Margaret read it: "God keep you. From your loving wife," she said. "What is the matter with it?" It had to be pointed out to her that a stop makes all the difference.

"During the war," says Bella, "an old lady who lived downstairs and had many letters to write, asked Mother if one of us would help her, as she herself could not write. Mother sent Margaret, and Margaret, always so ready to help anyone in difficulties, went at once. She thought the old lady would write simple little letters like Mother, but when she began she

used so many big words that Margaret was not sure how to spell them. ' It is a great humiliation,' she said afterwards, ' for I am young, and this generation has had a good education. It was very different when she was young, and many people did not go to school at all.' When the old lady got ill, Margaret went to see her in the infirmary. She used to go to see any sick person if she thought they would like a visit.

" Margaret was not gifted intellectually beyond the average girl of her age and circumstances of life," says Father A——, S.J., her spiritual director during the last years of her life in the world. " There are a number of small colour-paintings of hers, a scene of Loch Lomond, some flowers, the Apparition at Lourdes, etc., which are a credit to her considering her total lack of training and the crude colours she had to use. Her letters and jottings are grammatically incorrect, and even misspelt sometimes, but they show a depth of thought and an understanding of the mysteries

of our holy faith, which surpass the average of even educated girls of her age."

"Even to the last," says her sister, "Margaret would never go out without first asking Mother if she might go. When she was ready to start she would say: 'Well, I'm away, Mother,' and if Mother did not answer, she would go back to see why."

"She was always cheerful and obedient to her father and mother," says her brother Andrew, "and a loving and understanding sister to us all. She had great influence on me, and brought it to bear when she thought I was not doing right."

During the war the two girls had allotments, in which they worked every evening, and Margaret, though she knew nothing of gardening, won a prize for vegetables and for the best-kept plot. "It is surprising," the other workers would say, "how everything succeeds with that girl." They went, too, to meetings for moss-picking for the soldiers at St. Anne's school, and her old schoolfellows who met her

there, speak of her as full of fun and laughter over the reminiscences of her schooldays.

"If I thought that I had done something that might have given pain to Mother," says Bella, "Margaret would say to me: 'Offer to do a little service for her; ask her, after tea, if you cannot wash up for her while she takes a little rest, or ask what you *can* do to help her.' She and I were always the best of friends; we got on so well together.

"After Holy Communion on Sundays, as that was the only day when Margaret was able to make her thanksgiving in quietness at home, she spent nearly all the time in devotion. She loved to sit in the quiet of our bedroom and meditate."

Yet Margaret was not without the difficulties and trials of other girls of her age and position. "When she had a temptation to do wrong," says Bella, "she would say 'JESUS' ten times slowly, thinking of the power of the Holy Name, and her temptation would pass away.

" At home, when the Angelus rang, or, on Sundays, the bell for the Elevation at Mass, she always stopped what she was doing. If the others were reading, or so much interested in what they were doing that they did not notice it, she would remind them. ' Hush,' she would say, ' I think that is the Angelus bell,' and then we would all say the Angelus together.''

The two girls used to go to the Convent of the Helpers of the Holy Souls in Drummond Place on certain evenings, to help with the mending of the Cathedral vestments. Margaret, who was good at needlework, learnt to do a little embroidery, and—to her delight —was allowed to mend the lace on the Bishop's rochet. " When she came to help to mend the altar linen," says one of the nuns, " she never chose the easiest work, but was ready for anything, and humbly allowed herself to be shown how to do it. The gentleness and affection of the two sisters for each other was very marked. Margaret loved hearing about the life of our

Lord, our Blessed Lady and the Saints, and we seldom spoke of anything else when they were alone with us. Though she knew nothing of religious life it was clear how strong was her attraction to a humble and hidden life spent in prayer."

The nuns would sometimes speak of the work of their Order in the mission field, and Margaret would listen with intense interest. "She often spoke of mission work," says Bella, " and liked everything connected with it. She was a member of the Society for the Propagation of the Faith, and never missed paying her contribution. In the end we got a book for our family, and all the names in it were Sinclair. She saved up her stamps for the missions, and we bought three babies—ours were yellow or brown, I don't remember which —but Mother's was right black. Margaret wanted to call all three of them Theresa, for she had a great devotion to the Little Flower, and was always talking of her simple, holy life. There was one prayer she used to say to

Margaret, with her Mother and Sister.

(Margaret is on her mother's right.)

her: 'O God, who didst inflame with Thy
Spirit of Love the soul of Thy servant Theresa,
grant that I may love Thee and make Thee
greatly loved.'

"She used to put sums of money in St.
Anthony's box, and send some to a home for
orphans. She had a lot of little pictures, and
on one of them was a prayer that she used often
to say: 'O loving St. Anthony, you whose
heart is ever full of loving sympathy, whisper
my prayers into the ears of the Infant Jesus,
Who loved to linger in your arms.'"

Simple reminiscences these, yet they give
us vivid little glimpses into the tender loving
soul of this humble working-girl, who thought
of everyone but herself and lived her life purely
for God.

When the two elder girls were both at work,
they used to go away together every summer
for their holiday. The first year they went to
Dundee where they had relations; the second
year, when Margaret was seventeen, they
went to Rosewell, and that, she always said,

was the most delightful holiday they ever had.

Rosewell is a little mining village close to the famous Roslin Chapel, built in the fifteenth century by the Sinclairs of Rosslyn to the glory of God, and pillaged in the seventeenth by a " godly " mob from Edinburgh, to the glory of " the Kirk." As a private chapel, it resisted the ravages of Knox and his " rascal multitude " longer than most Catholic places of worship, but is now in Protestant hands. The descendants of those who had lavished their wealth or their labour on this beautiful setting for the Jewel of the Blessed Sacrament, driven out, like their Master, by aliens, worshipped Him until quite recent times in a ruinous barn where Rosewell now stands. There are people still living who remember Mass being said there, while one of the congregation held an umbrella over the head of the officiating priest. A tiny outhouse on one side was used alternately as a confessional or a stable for the priest's horse. When the Sinclairs went there,

a chapel-school had been built, and Mass was said there every morning.

" That was a real holiday," Margaret would often say, for they lodged in a tiny cottage away in the heart of the country. " It was like heaven, far from the sound of trams and buses —perfect silence excepting for the singing of birds and the rustling of the trees in the breeze." " Is it not lovely? " she would say to Bella. " Is not God good and wonderful? " " And then," says Bella, " she would give a little sigh, as if she would like to fly away somewhere where she would be at peace for ever."

They lived with an old couple in a very poor little cottage on a large estate, more than a mile from any other house. They arrived on a Saturday night, and, as soon as they had unpacked and had their tea, Margaret, as usual, proposed that they should go to find the chapel, to learn at what hour Mass would be said on the following day. On the way back she suggested to Bella that they should both

go to Mass and Communion every day while they were there. Bella objected. To Mass, perhaps, but not to Communion—she was not good enough. "It is the devil that is putting that into your head," was the prompt rejoinder. "Since you go on the first Friday, on Saturday and Sunday, and often at other times—why not for the whole week?" Bella persisted that she could not keep it up for a whole week. "Then," she says, "Margaret talked to me very seriously, and when she had finished she had me well converted. So we never missed one morning all the time we were there. 'When you begin to go,' she said, 'you will find out that you cannot live without it.' And so it was—thanks to dear little Margaret. 'You are not going because you are good,' she used to say, 'but because you want to try to be good.'"

At the end of the week the priest in charge, who had noticed the two girls, sent the little altar boy round after Mass to ask them to speak to him in the sacristy. "He was a very big

man," says Bella, " and he talked to us gravely, with one hand on Margaret's shoulder and one on mine." He asked them where they came from, and said that they were good girls and that they must go on, and keep up their practice of Holy Communion. " We were very happy," says Bella, " but we felt like sinking right down under the ground."

" After breakfast Margaret would sit—or kneel—outside in the open air, reading the prayers of thanksgiving in her prayer-book. She never seemed to get tired. She often spoke of the Holy Family, of their poverty and their happiness. ' Think what convent life must be like,' she would say, ' when country life is so happy.' She was so happy that you would really think that she had found a great treasure. ' How lovely it is here,' she would say, ' away from all the noise of the world and all its temptations.' "

The water for the needs of the household was obtained from an old draw-well in a field about fifty yards from the cottage. The two

E

girls would go and fetch it, singing through the summer morning, with all their hearts, the hymns that they knew best. Then they would do the washing-up for the old people and most of the housework. When Mrs. Sinclair came down one day with Lizzie to see " the loveliness of it all," the old lady was loud in their praise. They would not let her do anything, she said, but were like two daughters to her. " What a happy mother you must be, to have two such children! " The village store was over a mile away, she said, and off they used to go every day to do her messages, " singing, hand in hand, like two happy children."

" Margaret took us to her favourite place," says Lizzie, " where she and Bella used to go and sit together and sing the little Office of the Children of Mary. There was a stream, with a little wooden bridge across it, sheltered from the heat of the sun."

Margaret's only regret was that there was no real church at Rosewell, but only the little school-chapel. A few years later, just before

The Cottage at Rosewell.

she became a nun, she had the great joy of
seeing Bishop Grey Graham lay the foundation
stone of the new church, dedicated to St.
Matthew, the patron saint of Roslin.

CHAPTER IV

ENGAGEMENT

" All is too little and insufficient, whatever Thou
bestowest upon me, that is not Thyself; and whatever
Thou revealest to me concerning Thyself, or promisest, as
long as I see Thee not nor fully possess Thee : because
indeed my heart cannot truly rest nor be entirely contented till it rest in Thee, above all Thy gifts and every
created thing."—*Imitation of Christ*, III, 21.

IN the summer of 1919, the two sisters
went for their holiday to Bo'ness, the name
bestowed by its inhabitants on the little sea-
port town of Borrowstounness, on the Firth of
Forth.   Beyond the fact that James Watt, the
engineer, tested his first steam-engine in one
of the now exhausted collieries of the place,
and that it is one of the most ancient seaports
of Scotland, there is not very much in Bo'ness
to interest a visitor, and Margaret was greatly

disappointed with it.   The noise and bustle of it all was too like Edinburgh, and she loved the heart of the country.   Relations of a friend who lived in the same house as the Sinclairs, offered them a room which delighted Margaret, a great lover of cleanliness, by its spotless purity.   Their hostess met the two girls at the station, and took them to tea with her sister-in-law, married to a Protestant, where they met her nephew, P—— L——, a young ex-service man, who, though a Catholic, had—like his aunt—ceased to practise his religion.   It was Saturday, and Margaret's first question, as usual, was about the Mass next day.   To her great astonishment no one could vouchsafe any information.

P—— was evidently much struck with Margaret.   " She had a lovely face," says one of her old school friends, who knew her well at this time, " with hair that waved of itself." The charm of her face seems to have lain chiefly in expression — but not altogether. " She was a very pretty girl," writes a friend

who knew her some years later, "and I liked to see her smiling face." Her sister tells us that many young men of her age would have been glad to "keep company" with her, but she would have none of them. Here, however, the case was different. P—— was evidently not living up to his duties as a Catholic, and there was a soul to be helped. He asked Margaret to go out with him, and she went, insisting, however, that Bella should be of the party. He bought sweets for the two girls and took them round the town to see the docks—the chief pride of the place. On the following Sunday he went to Mass with them, and they had a long talk afterwards. Margaret spoke seriously to him, says Bella, about his way of speaking and his constant use of the Holy Name. P—— declared that it was only a bad habit that he had fallen into; he did it almost unconsciously; it would be very hard to stop it.

Margaret replied that it gave her much pain to hear him. He then said that, if she would

keep company with him, he would really try to do better.

"I must say," says Bella, "he really did try, for he wanted her very much to keep company with him." Margaret told him that he would have to change very much first, and he set to work earnestly to do so. When the improvement was really manifest, she allowed him to go and see her father and mother. She also suggested that he should become a Knight of the Blessed Sacrament, as she thought he would find it very helpful. After considering the matter, he decided to follow her advice. Margaret was delighted, and still more delighted when he became very zealous over it and began to enrol others. "She was pleased," says Bella, "more for the good of his soul and the glory of God than for anything else, though she always felt very sorry for him, living as he did, among non-Catholics and people who had not much faith. He kept it up very well, and the priest at Bo'ness thought a good deal of him. He had him in

the choir, and he was at the head of the boy-
scouts. When he heard that he was thinking
of getting married, he asked to see the girl,
and when he saw Margaret, he said to her:
'I hope you are a good girl, for P—— is a
very good boy.' He asked her if she went to
Mass, and many other questions."

Margaret answered him simply, without
letting him suspect the state of the case, or
that P—— owed his new-born zeal to her
influence. Although she had told P——
several times that she had no intention of
marrying him, he thought that she was joking,
and did not believe her. She was gradually
drifting against her own inclinations into
something very like a definite engagement.
"Mammy," she said one day to her mother,
"it may be that he will lose his soul; I'd
rather make the sacrifice than that."

The following summer the sisters went
for their holiday to a country place, a little
distance from Bo'ness, where P—— used
frequently to cycle out to see them.

"He gave Margaret a present of a locket and chain," says Bella, "but she liked much better one that Mother had given her. P—— put his photograph in the one he gave her, so Margaret put Mother's in the other side, otherwise I don't think she would have worn it. At times she put it on, and when some of the girls, who were rather curious, would ask her to open it, she would just smile, and then they would open it themselves. Of course they all knew Mother, for she was always with us— although Mother did not know half of them —but they did not know P——, and she never used to tell them who he was. She listened calmly to them as they guessed, but she never made anyone the wiser.

"He was always very nice to Mother and Father, and all of us. When we were at Bo'ness we used to go to the pictures with him, but not without his aunt and his friends. Margaret never left me to go with him. Sometimes I tried to slip away unnoticed, but whenever she missed me she was after me.

Mother and Father thought that, if she liked him, he was a very good match, for he was a good Catholic now, such as any girl might have been glad to marry.

" We liked," says Bella, " when the weather was fine, to go away on Saturday or Sunday for the day. Mother loved to go for a drive on the top of the car, away into the country or down to the sea, and Margaret used to find out all the nice places that she thought it would give her pleasure to visit. Sometimes P—— would come in on those days, without writing to say that he was coming. 'He can just go home again,' Margaret would say, 'for we have it all arranged to go out with Mother.' Mother would declare that we could easily put off our trip till another day, but Margaret would rather disappoint P—— ten times than Mother once. She would leave him sitting in the room alone, or, if she could, would put him off on to John or Andrew, to keep him in conversation.

" John was not pleased with her for behaving

Margaret, with her Father and Sister.

Margaret is in the middle.

in that way; he would say that it was a shame to treat P—— like that. Mother was very glad when it came to an end, for Margaret was really in torture, and Mother had begun to waken up to the fact. A kind of shiver would come over her when she was told to go out with him. 'You should tell him plainly that you do not want him,' said Mother. 'I did,' said Margaret, 'but he said he would do away with himself if I threw him over.'

"When she was alone with me, she used to cry and say: 'Oh dear, it is awful!' I tried to comfort her, but she would answer: 'It is all right for you, but you do not know what a sacrifice it would be to me.'"

Margaret's father and mother grew anxious, yet they did not quite know what to do. Knowing how wise she was, they concluded that it would be best to leave her to manage her own affairs, without interfering in any way. "She thought," says her sister, "that if she broke her engagement off, she would give us all great pain, and rather than do that,

she would make the sacrifice and go through with it, although it would be like martyrdom to her. Mother asked her at last why she had kept on with it for so long. ' I thought it was the will of God,' said Margaret, ' and that I might grow to like him.' "

It was probably the growing—though half unconscious—realization of a religious vocation that was causing Margaret's misery. She went at last, in despair, to see Father A——, a Jesuit priest to whom she had been going to confession, and asked him if it would be a sin to break off an engagement. It depended on circumstances, he said.

Father A—— was much impressed with Margaret's perfect simplicity and absolute lack of self-consciousness. She sat in one of the little parlours at Lauriston, facing the window, with the light full on her face, and, though the tears were in her eyes, told him the whole story with a calmness and restraint that was very striking. Though many girls would have been nervous under the questioning to

Church of the Sacred Heart, Lauriston.

Photo, Fairer.

which he necessarily submitted her, she was completely at her ease. " What she had done for P—— was a great act of charity, but, under the circumstances, she was in no way bound to marry him," was the decision of Father A——. He advised, however, that on account of her youth, she should think the matter well over, lest later she might regret her action. Her reply convinced him that there was no danger of this, and Margaret, greatly consoled and comforted, went home and wrote the following letter :

" DEAR P——,—Time changes all things on this earth, so if you pay attention to that first line you will not think so much of the following. I must tell you that I am still of the same opinion as on Sunday. I really wish to break with it because I know I do not care for you. You understand when we first met it was different, because the circumstances made it so. I was rather moved by your position then, as it was not the best. I have

done what God inspired me to do, to help you, the little I could, to regain the Light. From that moment, God and His Blessed Mother must have showered down their blessing on you, because you have remained steadfast since, and I trust in God that you will continue doing so, because you know He is the only real happiness. . . . You will recollect a year ago, I wrote a similar letter to this, but when you came, you implored of me not to. I must be rather chicken-hearted, because I agreed, but I feel I *cannot* let it go on any longer. Perhaps you will be hurt at my saying this, but if you take a broad view of it you will see it is better now than after."

P—— evidently *was* hurt, and perhaps surprised, but he seems to have realized that Margaret was thoroughly in earnest. He sent her back the beads and prayer-book, etc., she had given him, and her letters—a needless precaution this, said Margaret, as there was nothing in them but good advice for his

soul. " Her conversation was generally about religion," he himself said later to Father A——, " telling me to go to my duties, etc. She allowed no flirting or walking arm in arm. I never dared to be familiar with her. What I admired was her faith. She made a new man of me."

CHAPTER V

VOCATION

" Have you not heard His silent steps ?
   He comes, comes, ever comes.
Every moment and every age, and every day and every
      night,
   He comes, comes, ever comes. . . .
In every song, in the fragrant days of sunny April,
      through the forest path . . . in the rainy gloom of
      July nights. . . . It is the golden touch of His feet
      that makes my joy to shine."
                                        —R.T.

WHEN Margaret was a child at school, a young companion who had noticed some of their schoolfellows kneeling longer at their prayers than the others, said, one day, laughingly : " I wonder what convent they will enter ? "

" I could never enter a convent," said Margaret, " I could never get up early enough in the morning."

Yet she had always a great love and admiration for the religious life. " She used to speak of certain nuns," says her sister, " and of how devout and cheerful they were." " I am sure," she would say—with an understanding beyond her years—" that they must do great penance, and that is why they are always laughing." She often declared that the beauty of their souls shone in their eyes—a remark that was frequently made, in after years, about herself. She liked to read of the Saints who had been rich and had worn sackcloth under their splendid garments.

It is difficult to know when Margaret first began to think seriously of her own religious vocation. It was certainly in her mind—if only subconsciously—during the later period of her engagement to P——. " I should like to enter a convent," she said one day to her sister, soon after the break, " I have seen something of life in the world, and, though I have enjoyed it, I do not think much of it. I do not think it is for me."

F

In the autumn that followed, she went with Bella to a retreat for working girls, given at the convent of Marie Réparatrice in Ferry Road. She made it very earnestly, says her sister, refusing to break the rule of silence even to greet old friends whom she had not seen for some time. "After every sermon," says Bella, "we went to the chapel for a quarter of an hour's meditation. Margaret was so still in her adoration, for the Blessed Sacrament was exposed every day, and she loved to stay there, as long as she could, on her knees."

It was probably during those hours of silent prayer that God's Holy Will was made clear to her, for from that time onwards her spiritual life seems to have grown deeper and fuller. "I never dared to say anything uncharitable when I was with her," says a friend of her girlhood. "I used to feel envious of her virtue and told her so, but she was not one that showed much of her religious nature, and she did not like to be praised. 'We can all become better by praying to God,' she said. I never had a

quarrel with her and never heard of anyone else having had one."

The same friend speaks of her sweetness and her readiness to do anything to help others. "One day," she says, "I admired a very pretty hat that she had made for herself. 'I wish I could make myself pretty hats like that,' I said. 'I will show you how,' she said instantly, and though I know she had an engagement that evening, she put it off to come home with me and teach me."

Margaret was working, at this time, in the biscuit factory of McVitie & Price in Robertson Avenue. She did her work—the french-polishing of the show-cases for their exhibits—in a little room by herself. "She always wore her H.B.S. brooch over her overall," says Bella, "and one day a Catholic girl, who came to her room to speak to her, asked her if she was not afraid to show her religion so openly. 'There is nothing to be afraid of in being a Handmaid of God,' answered Margaret quietly.

"She never talked to anyone unless it was

necessary," says her sister, " but she had a kind smile of recognition for all. She took her prayer-book and beads with her to work, and kept them on the little table beside her." One day a joiner, who was working in the same establishment, came into the room and told her the kind of story that is too common in factories. Margaret neither moved nor raised her eyes. He came in again, another day, but seeing her with her prayer-book and rosary on the table before her, went out again quickly, and told the other men to keep out of that room. He began to make inquiries soon afterwards about the Catholic religion, and had a Mass said that he might do what was right.

"Everyone treated her with respect in the places where she worked," says her brother Andrew. "She had the sweetest nature, and was full of consideration for others. She was wholly unselfish, and always willing and ready to oblige everyone. I never saw her show temper."

Bella, on the other hand, had difficulties

with her temper. It was not always under control, and she sometimes looked rather glum. " Margaret used to tell me," she frankly avers, " that sometimes I looked anything but pleasant, and, of course, everyone told me the same thing. But Margaret would comfort me. ' When you see any of the other girls,' she would say, ' just force yourself to give a little smile, no matter how you are feeling. For sometimes they may be just waiting for you to give a smile first, or they may be in difficulties or out of sorts. You never know who may be in trouble, and when you give them a smile in passing, it may lighten the way for them and give them courage to bear it.' "

We have here the secret of Margaret's own smile—so " irresistible " and " winning "—of which everyone who knew her seems to have such a vivid remembrance. Begun for the love of God, it became at last so habitual that it never left her lips—even amidst the agonies of her last most painful illness. It was a smile that uplifted the hearts of others and spoke to

them of heaven—for it was the perfect homage of her soul to God.

"I used to say to her," says Bella, "I shall never be like you, for you are so wise and so clever, and I have such a lot of faults. 'You have no more faults than I,' she would say, but I knew that was not the case. She told me to pray to the Holy Ghost for wisdom, for she often prayed for that herself. I asked her what she thought of my temper. 'You are not really bad-tempered,' she would say, 'but only a little impatient.' I used often to wonder how she could be so nice to me and so quick to forgive when I had been disagreeable, and I sometimes said so to her. 'One of us must make an act of humility,' she said, 'and you won't.'"

Bella was thinking of joining the Little Sisters of the Poor. "Mother used to tell me," she says, "that I should have to change a great deal first or I should make all the old people afraid of me. Then Margaret would say: 'Well, Mother, God will give her the grace to fight against it.' One day I asked

St. Cuthbert's Church, Slateford, where Margaret used to spend her dinner hour.

her: ' If Father A—— were to ask you in
confession if you would be a nun, what would
you say?' ' Oh,' she cried in a voice full of
joy, ' I should go at once; I should not put it
off for a minute.'"

Though those of her own family looked up
to Margaret and always went to her for help
and sympathy, outsiders, owing to her reserve
and habit of putting herself in the background,
often thought that the elder sister, who was
very bright and merry, was the more gifted of
the two.

It was a long way from Blackfriars Street to
Robertson Avenue, where Margaret went to
work, and sometimes when Mass was over she
had no time for breakfast. She used to take
her dinner with her, but not infrequently
brought it back with her when she came home
at night. Her mother protested, but Margaret
would laugh and say that she liked best dining
at home. She loved the beautiful little church
of St. Cuthbert's at Slateford, which was quite
close to the factory where she worked, and she

used often to go there to spend her dinner-hour in prayer. "She often spoke," says Bella, "of the children of St. Cuthbert's school—how well-mannered and devout they were. They would come in—even the tiny ones—to make the Way of the Cross, or for a visit to the Blessed Sacrament. The little boys were so polite and manly, she said, taking off their caps, or saluting as they passed before the door of the church, while the little girls would genuflect or make the sign of the Cross. She used to like to stop and speak to them."

A Sister from one of the neighbouring convents relates how, when she was passing near St. Cuthbert's one day, carrying a heavy bag, a hand suddenly seized on it from behind, and turning, she saw the sweet face of a young girl smiling over her shoulder. "Let me carry that, Sister," she said. The Sister refused, and they compromised by carrying it together. "I asked her then," says the Sister, "if one could get into the church, as I often passed it, but I thought the door was locked." "Oh,

Side Door of St. Cuthbert's Church.
(Close to the School Playground.)

she said, "there is a side door that is always
open; I go in often for a visit. I was just going
in now."

The two went in together. "I was much
struck," says the Sister, "by her reverence and
devotion, and when we came out she offered
to help me carry the bag a little farther."
They walked on together, talking, and in the
course of conversation the Sister asked
Margaret if she had ever thought of the
Religious Life. She flushed and was silent.
"Perhaps there is some other attraction,"
suggested the Sister, and began to speak of
something else. Margaret told her that she
was a french-polisher, and suggested that, if
there was anything, at any time, that she could
do for the nuns in that way, she would be very
glad to come out after her working hours and
do it. There happened to be a table that
required treatment, and Margaret promised to
come one evening and polish it. They then
parted, and the Sister as she went home thought
with much interest of her new acquaintance.

Margaret kept her promise, but as she worked till six o'clock at McVitie's, by the time she had gone back to Blackfriars Street, taken her evening meal and reached the convent, some way out of the city, it was too late to begin. The Sister took her to the convent garden, where they sat talking together about the happiness of religious life, while the sun set in glory over the Pentlands. " This is like heaven," said Margaret.

That summer the two sisters went for their holiday to Loch Lomond, and this time Lizzie went with them. It was a holiday after Margaret's own heart, and the youngest sister was rather surprised to see how she took the lead in everything. Margaret was very fond of pictures, and proposed that they should break their journey at Glasgow to go to the Art Gallery. She made all the necessary inquiries—for none of them knew where it was—deposited their belongings in the left luggage office, and started off. The two others declared that she would certainly end

by losing them, and that they would never get
to their journey's end. "You will be there in
time for tea," said Margaret. "She was very
much interested in everything she saw in the
Art Gallery," says Lizzie, "and asked many
questions of the attendant—and we *did* arrive
safely at our journey's end—and we *were* in
time for tea."

On the next morning—Sunday—after Mass,
the three girls set forth to find a place from
which they had been told that, if they climbed
to a little height, they would get a most beautiful view of the Loch. They then came down
to the shore and sat down on a great stone to
rest. "Let us sing a hymn to our Blessed
Lady," said Margaret. Lizzie protested that
there were people sitting on a bench not far
away, but Margaret began to sing and Bella
joined in. The echo of their fresh young
voices came back to them across the Loch.
"How beautiful this is," said Margaret, "the
Loch in front of us and the woods behind;
God's own nature." They went on several

sailing expeditions—one to Luss—where they found falls and salmon leaping in the sun—" a thing we had never seen before." They went to Rothesay, and the adventurous Margaret even hired a boat. " It was rather a risk," says Bella, " for we did not know how to row." Lizzie, who valued her life, refused to get in. " But when we got home," says Bella, " we went to Craiglockhart ponds with Mother, who loves boating too."

At Rothesay, they went to the church for a visit, but found it closed for repairs. The priest's housekeeper, however, let them in. " I am sure we were there for two hours," says Bella, " for the girl came several times to close the door, but as we were making the Way of the Cross, she left us alone. We had our little books with us, and Margaret read the prayers out loud so that I could follow them, and I answered the Pater, Ave and Gloria. We were very happy at having the chapel so long to ourselves."

" One day," says Bella, " when Margaret

Margaret Sinclair.

(From a Photograph taken at Rothesay.)

was attending a course of sermons at the Church of the Sacred Heart, Lauriston, the preacher spoke about the Convent of Poor Clares at Liberton. The nuns were in great need of succour, he said, as they had often nothing to eat. After that, Mother was so sorry for them that we used to go out on Thursday or Saturday if the weather was fine, for we had those two afternoons free every week.

" At the back of the chapel of the Poor Clares there are many little boxes. Needless to say, Margaret had many intentions, and she would choose which boxes she would put something into. One day she said to me: ' I should love to be a Poor Clare.' "

CHAPTER VI

LAST MONTHS AT HOME

" In Thy gift shall we rest; there shall we enjoy Thee, our rest, our place. Love lifts us up thither, and Thy good Spirit exalts our humbleness from the gates of death. In good will is our peace. The body by its own weight, strives towards its own place. Weight is not downward only, but to its own place. Fire tends upward, a stone downward. . . .

" My weight is my love; by that I am borne whithersoever I am borne. By Thy Gift we are inflamed and are borne upward; we are kindled, and we go. We ascend by the ascents in our heart, and sing a song of degrees; by Thy fire—by Thy good fire are we kindled and we go, for we go upward to the peace of Jerusalem."

—St. Augustine.

It was not long before Margaret told her sister that she had spoken to Father A——
about her vocation, and had expressed to him her desire to be a Poor Clare. She did not

tell her, however, that he had laid the difficulty and the austerity of the life very clearly before her, and that, to the question: " Will you be able to bear it? " she had answered: " With God's help, yes."

Margaret went to the convent at Liberton to ask the Mother Abbess if she would accept her as an Extern Sister, but she was told that there were already four girls waiting to enter there. The Mother Abbess would have taken her as an Intern Sister, but this she declined. She may have been moved by humility, or she may have thought that, as Father A—— had told her to offer herself as an Extern Sister, it was best to do exactly as she was told. Father A—— was then under the impression that the Extern Sisters of the Poor Clares might, as in the Carmelite Order, be admitted later on to the enclosure, if they desired it and it was thought advisable. He learnt later that this was not so.

The Mother Abbess at Liberton told Margaret that there might be a chance for her

if she applied at the Poor Clare Convent at Notting Hill, and this she eventually did.

Bella had already declared her vocation for the Little Sisters of the Poor. Since they were both for the religious life, she said to herself, why not for the same Order? "I asked her," she says, "to come with me, and be a Little Sister of the Poor, for I thought I could not live without her; but she was firm. She had made up her mind to join the Poor Clares. She asked me what I would think of that for myself, but I said that it was all right for those that liked it, but not for me." We had many long conversations about it when we were together, and Father often asked us what all the whispering was about. I am sure he and Mother would have liked if we had both entered the same Order, and that it added to Mother's pain that we were separated, but it was the Will of God.

"It was Margaret who saved my vocation," she says, "for she was so wise and she advised me in such a motherly way that I could have

Margaret's Room, showing her little altar.

listened to her all day. She never tired me. When first I told her that my confessor had spoken to me twice upon the subject, and that I was not going back to him, she told me how foolish this was. She made me afraid, for she said that it was a serious thing to refuse such a grace from God, and that I would never have any luck if I had a vocation and did not respond to it. I asked her to pray for me that I might do so. I could always offer myself, she said; though it was one thing to offer and another to be accepted. Of course Father and Mother knew what we were thinking of, but I don't think they knew that we had decided to take the step.

" She told me that, as I was going to enter in June, she had suggested to Father A—— that, for Mother's sake, she should wait till the end of the year, but he had advised her not to do so, as, though it would be a great blow to Father and Mother, to wait would be only to prolong it."

So Margaret broke the news to her mother.

G

Though Mrs. Sinclair had given her eldest daughter generously to God, the certainty that He was asking for Margaret too, was for the moment more than she could bear. She could not give her consent, she said, just then. She would go to Mass and Communion first. When she came back, strength had been given her for the sacrifice, and she told Margaret that she could go where God was calling her.

"Margaret had to go to her work rather early to catch the train or 'bus," says Bella, "and Mother used to get things ready for her, when she came home from Mass. Sometimes she had no time to come in; she would hear the 'bus coming, and off she would go, rather than be late for her work. One morning—I think the priest must have overslept himself—there was no Mass. Margaret was beginning to lose hope, and while she prayed, I went to the sacristy to ask about it. It was too late now, the priest said, for it was almost time for the second Mass; but he would give Holy Communion. When I went back to tell

Margaret this, she was delighted—she was not going to be disappointed after all. It was her last minute and she had been praying with all her heart. She could not remain in the church for her thanksgiving, nor go home for breakfast, but had to go at once to her work. When I went home everything was on the table just as Mother had left it, even Margaret's dinner, that she was to have taken with her. I am quite sure she had nothing to eat all that day, till she came home at night. When she was at Mass, after receiving Holy Communion, she was so full of love for our dear Blessed Lord in the Sacrament of the Altar, that she never knew when the last Gospel had come, but knelt on, without moving."

The three girls slept in the same room, and Lizzie relates that often, when she woke up in the night, she would see Margaret, kneeling with outstretched arms on the floor, praying. One night her mother, having left something in the girls' room, came in and saw

the white figure kneeling there motionless, absorbed in prayer. She did not hear the door open, nor notice that anyone had entered. Mrs. Sinclair, awestricken, crept out, closing the door softly behind her. She never went into the girls' room at night again.

The mother's awe was not surprising. She knew that Margaret was of the temperament that requires a good deal of sleep, and that early rising had always been a difficulty to her. Her brother, when asked to mention what faults he had noticed in his sister, could think of none, save her tendency to sleep. In the evening, when friends came in to see them, she would sometimes fall asleep in her chair, or would be so unable to keep awake that she would have to leave them and go to bed. When she went to St. Cuthbert's, to spend her dinner hour in prayer, she would sometimes— from sheer weariness — fall asleep in the church. When one remembers that french-polishing is a fairly strenuous occupation and that Margaret's working hours were from eight

Margaret Sinclair.

(From a Photograph taken just before she became a Poor Clare.)

in the morning to six at night, that she was tired is not surprising. Under the circumstances, her deliberate choice of the life of a Poor Clare, and the nightly vigils with which she prepared herself for it, has something in it of heroism.

When Margaret mentioned to one of the Sisters of the Convent of Mercy, who had taught her as a child, that she was going to enter with the Poor Clares, the Sister asked her if it were not a very hard life. " I have been practising," said Margaret simply, " for some time past."

She made a little cross of wood, polished it carefully, and inserted in it eight sharp nails, with the points sticking out. This she wore, bound round her body with string, so that the points pierced her back. Mrs. R——, an intimate friend of whom she was very fond, and who used often to go with her to Mass in the mornings, had the habit of patting her sometimes, in friendly fashion, on the back. One day, as she did this, Margaret flinched.

" Are you in pain," asked her friend anxiously.
" No, no," said Margaret quickly. " And to
think it was I," said Mrs. R—— later, " who
drove those nails into her innocent flesh!"
After Margaret's death, her mother gave the
little cross to Mrs. R——. These relics
are now in the possession of the committee
engaged on the investigation of her cause.

The same friend says of Margaret that,
when told of any trouble or difficulty, she
would always answer : " Offer it all up to the
Heart of Jesus." She would then close her
eyes and, smiling, clasp her hands in prayer.
It was her cure for every evil. She had great
devotion to the Sacred Heart, and always,
after Mass or Benediction, used to kneel and
pray before the Sacred Heart altar. One
feast day when it was very beautifully
decorated, Mrs. R—— asked her if she liked
it. " It is lovely," she said, and then with
great sorrow, " but I wish the Sacred Heart
was more loved."

" Do you not think that Margaret Sinclair is

too much thought of?" asked an acquaintance not long ago of Mrs. R——.

"Did you know her?" was the quiet answer.

"No." It was enough.

Margaret used often to say, says her sister, that she would not live long. Her mother thought that she was only trying to make them laugh, for she looked fresh and healthy. But Margaret was quite serious. "I do not want to live long," she would say to Bella, when they were alone, "and I cannot think of myself living to old age."

In the April before she entered the Poor Clares, Margaret made another retreat at the convent of Marie Réparatrice.

"This was the only time I saw her," writes one of the nuns. "I noticed a retreatant, after the afternoon instruction, kneeling motionless in the front bench in the chapel. About half an hour later I looked in again. She was there still, kneeling in the same place, and I was struck by her expression. Her eyes were fixed on the monstrance; there was more than

faith in them—it must have been almost
vision. In deep reverence I closed the door,
feeling that I had been the witness of a divine
secret. A few moments later the bell rang
for tea, and the girl came out of the chapel.
As she passed, I asked one of the other nuns
who was standing near me, who she was.
' Margaret Sinclair,' was the answer.

" I watched her at tea, and noticed the quiet,
unselfish way in which she looked after the
wants of the other girls and how she helped
to clear away afterwards. I could not help
thinking that that was genuine piety. The
next day I met her in the garden and spoke a
few words to her, but she did not say much.
She was a silent girl, but I noticed her lovely
eyes—' eyes that saw visions,' as one of her
girl-friends said.

" She loved the quiet of the garden and the
shrine of Our Lady of Lourdes, but above
all the chapel, with the Blessed Sacrament
exposed. I also knew that it was through her
example and her sweet influence that one of

her girl-friends found courage to break off her engagement with a Protestant. It was a hard struggle at the time, but she too, later, was to hear the call of the Divine Lover, and she is now a fervent novice."

"She came a few times to our guild for business girls," says another nun of the same convent. "She was a singularly quiet and unassuming girl, yet there was something about her which gave one an impression of peace — something indescribable, which brought one's mind unconsciously back to her. A face angelic, fair, with large blue eyes, still and calm, reflecting a soul in touch with the beyond. At the guild she took part with the other members, quietly, but with interest. Her reserved manner had nothing distant about it. All the girls liked her. Her regret was that, living far away, she could not make it a regular practice to attend the weekly meetings.

"Our retreats brought her to us for two week-ends, at different intervals. The

second, in April, 1923, was the last she made before entering the Poor Clares. It was a retreat perfectly made. Silent and recollected, she was an example to all, yet everything was most simply done, with no exaggeration. Most of her time was spent before the Blessed Sacrament, exposed every day from Mass at half-past seven to Benediction at half-past five.

"She would kneel immovable, her eyes riveted on the white Host enthroned in the golden rays of the monstrance. Margaret, who chose to spend her holiday with her God, will inspire many souls to do the same."

By this time, Margaret, acting on Father A——'s advice, had written to the Reverend Mother Abbess of the Convent of Poor Clare Colettines at Notting Hill, asking to be admitted as an Extern Sister. The Mother Abbess wrote to Father A—— that she was agreeably impressed by Margaret's letter, but that she wished it to be explained to her that the life of a Poor Clare was one of very great

austerity. She also asked that she should be examined by a reliable doctor, in order to see whether she were fitted for such a life.

As Margaret had a slight cough, Father A—— proposed that she should go first for a fortnight's rest and change to the convalescent home at Lanark, managed by the Sisters of Charity. Before she went, she gave notice to her employers, who offered her an increase of wages and a holiday, during which they would keep her place vacant, if she would only remain with them. She explained that she was going away for altogether and was not coming back, took leave of them and went to Lanark. There she spent a happy fortnight, during which she paid a visit to the famous grotto of Our Lady of Lourdes at Carfin. She then returned home, and was examined by Dr.——, a well-known physician of Edinburgh, who pronounced her perfectly sound and quite fit for the life that she had chosen.

In July, just a month after Bella had left

home to join the Little Sisters of the Poor in their convent in Liverpool, where she was to make her postulate, Margaret started for London with her brother Andrew, bound for Canada. The poor mother within a few weeks had to part with three of her children, but she and her husband, convinced that they were doing the Will of God, offered them with generous hearts.

Margaret took her brother to Tilbury Docks, where she saw him off in the great steamer, and then went straight to Notting Hill. " It seems to me," says a priest who knew her there, " that her sanctity was assured before she saw the convent, and her life there was the test of its stability."

CHAPTER VII

IN THE CONVENT

" There He showed a fair and delectable place, and large enough for all mankind that shall be saved, and rest in peace and in love. And with the sweet beholding He showed His blessed Heart cloven in two . . . and the endless Love that was without beginning, and is, and ever shall be.

" And with this our good Lord said blessedfully : ' Lo, how I love thee,' as if He had said : ' My darling, behold and see the Lord thy God that is thy Maker, and thy endless Joy. See thine own Brother, thy Saviour. My child, behold and see what liking and bliss I have in thy salvation. And for My love enjoy with Me.'

" This showed our good Lord to make us glad and merry."—JULIAN OF NORWICH.

THE chapter on Margaret's convent life has yet to be written. We can only catch a few glimpses from her family and from the few of her letters that still survive.

" My Dear Parents," she wrote in September 1923, two months after her entrance, " I believe you have been greatly favoured with a letter from our Reverend Mother Abbess. I know, Mother dear, you would be delighted to have it, so now, dear Father and Mother, you must pray for me very sincerely that God will give me all the graces necessary to be a good religious. I am looking forward to my Clothing, so now, dear Mother, you must not let your spirits down, although you are not in good health at present, but you must look after yourself and get well and strong to come to London and see Isabella and I.

" I wish you a very happy birthday on the 25th, so I might wish Father the same, in case I am too busy to write before the 21st October. May God bless you both. Your ever loving child."

A letter to her youngest sister followed. In it one can see her loving solicitude for her

mother, deprived of the companionship of
her two elder daughters. "As she is the
youngest," she said to one of the Sisters of
Charity at Warley, "she has perhaps been a
little spoilt, and she might not be so thoughtful for Mother."

"MY DEAR LITTLE SISTER LIZZIE," she
wrote, "I have no doubt you are very busy
as well as troubled, but I venture to ask you
something, and I know you will do your best,
as well as Nellie (her sister-in-law), John and
Lawrence—that is to try and help dear Mother
as much as you can in every way, and also in
trying to cheer her up. My dear child Lizzie,
how often I think about you and pray to your
patron saint to give you something suitable
to do, so as you could be with dear Mother
more. This is just a wee note for yourself,
with much love from your devoted sister.
Pray for me."

In a letter to the family, she writes:

"DEAR SISTERS AND BROTHERS,—This is a picture of our garden. (Enclosed was a little photograph, reproduced here.) That tree is on the piece of ground I look after. It is a beautiful apple tree. I am sure this will make Lawrence quite keen on coming to see me.

"The window I mark X is our little cell. It is the sweetest place imaginable. How I love it.

"I am delighted to hear you had a letter from Isabella; be sure and tell her I send her my love. Sorry I am unable to write a longer letter. I wish to be remembered to Mrs. R——. With best love to John and Nellie, Lizzie, Lawrence, and wee Ella and Tizzie (her little nieces). God bless you all."

Another long letter contains the description of festivities on the feast of the Profession of her Mother Abbess, when the Extern Sisters had gone into the enclosure. "I never experienced such joy," she says, "as to be present

Corner of the Convent Garden, showing
Margaret's little apple tree.

when our Mother Abbess renewed her vows. The Blessed Sacrament being exposed all the time, and the clear voice of Mother Abbess sounding her vows to God; the heavenliness of it all. One could imagine Our Blessed Lord and Our Lady smiling down, and all the choir of angels rejoicing. I shall never forget that day, it was so good of Our Blessed Lord to allow poor wee me to be present."

She goes on to describe a little treat that had been given to the Sisters by someone who knew the convent. She knew that her mother was fretting a little over the austerities of her new life, and carefully emphasizes this little enjoyment. "Some of the enclosed Sisters," she says, at the end of her letter, " have never seen a motor-car or a bicycle, having been in the Cloister for over fifty years. You can hardly imagine anyone living in London who has never seen a motor; still, it is so of these dear old saints, living their life of penance and prayer, and all with such happiness."

A little later she wrote to Father A——,

H

telling him how happy she was and how amused at many things in her new life. "If you only knew all the quaint things we have to do on account of Holy Poverty," she said, "you would laugh outright." It pleased him to know that she could see the humorous side of the hard life she was leading.

In a little notebook, sent after her death to her mother, she chronicles her own Clothing in February, 1924, at which her mother, father and eldest brother were present. There was another joyful surprise in store for her. Bella, who had finished her postulate in Liverpool, was to go to France to make her novitiate. On the way, she came to the convent of her Order in London, just at the time of Margaret's Clothing.

"Margaret was in her bridal dress, sitting with Father and Mother and John," says Lizzie, "when the door opened, and Bella came in with two of her Sisters." The two fell into each other's arms. They were all present at the Clothing, which followed

immediately afterwards. Margaret was radiant—" like a happy child."

Her father, mother and brother spent the day at the convent, and Bella was allowed to remain with them. Margaret came to them, smiling and happy in her religious habit, and sat with them while they had dinner—" a magnificent dinner." During the rest of the day when they were talking to Margaret, she would suddenly say : " You must go and talk to Bella now, or she will be lonely." When they were talking to Bella, after a time she would interrupt them with : " Oh, do go and talk to Margaret now, for a little while." Each was thinking of the other.

Margaret told them about the little apple tree in the convent garden, of which she had been given charge. It was apparently dying and had seemed in a hopeless condition, but she had coaxed it into bearing blossoms. Later, when she was at Warley, it bore fruit.

The next entry in the little notebook is the death of her father, through a motor accident,

in the following December. We can imagine
with what love and sorrow she offered the
sacrifice to God, thinking more of her mother's
loneliness than of her own grief.

Was there any premonition of what lay
before her in a little prayer on the Stations of
the Cross, written shortly before her Profession? "Second Station. Jesus receives
the heavy Cross to carry. O my Jesus, you
accept it with patience and resignation, as you
desired our Redemption. You think not of
the suffering it will cost you or your Immacu-
late Mother, but only of saving us poor
miserable sinners from the abyss of hell. O
my God, help me always to take up Thy
cross cheerfully and follow Thee. . . . Holy
Mother, pierce me through, in my heart each
wound renew of my Saviour crucified."

Her resolutions of retreat for 1925 follow:

" I will be submissive in all things, always
having before me that my Lord, my God, was
ever submissive to St. Joseph and obedient
even until the death of the Cross. I will

Margaret Sinclair, as a Novice.

practise charity in my words and ever look out for little opportunities to perfect this beautiful virtue in helping my Sisters, especially in those things that are contrary to my nature. I will endeavour to be diligent, always to try and do all things well, and ever to have a pure intention in what I do. This year, please God, I desire to vow to You my poverty, chastity and obedience, and, to observe the same, to rejoice when I feel the pinch of poverty. And always to remain modest and prudent, thinking of this in our Blessed Lady, and how she would like it in her child."

Margaret Sinclair — now Sister Mary Francis of the Five Wounds—made her Religious Profession on the 14th of February, 1925. None of her family could be present— probably owing to the recent death of her father—but a friend who was there writes as follows :

" She looked lovely—there is no other word for it. When she was going over to the

Mother Abbess to receive her crown, she looked up at Our Blessed Lord with an unearthly look, and a smile that seemed to say : ' O my Lord, I belong to You at last.' A friend who was with me said as we went home : ' I shall never forget that look on Sister Mary Francis's face.' Others noticed it too."

"When passing through London," says a Franciscan priest, " I met Sister Francis a few times at the Colettine Convent, and was much impressed by her radiant appearance; she looked so guileless, simple, sincere, unaffected, docile and humble. This impression was antecedent to what I have since heard from her Sisters in religion regarding her saintly patience during her stay in the Sanatorium at Warley. . . . The impression was as lasting as it was instantaneous. . . .

" I think it rather remarkable that a man of my years—I am now in my seventy-second year—who is not at all impressionable, should be so wonderfully impressed. For we priests

meet many saintly souls. . . . Sister Francis, however, had a personality which made one *feel* that he was in the presence of unexampled candour of soul."

One of Sister Francis's duties, as an Extern Sister, was to go out questing for the convent, a practice of poverty which—with its possibilities of rebuff—is not pleasant to nature. Several people whom she visited during this time have mentioned her sunny cheerfulness, her sweet simplicity and her winning smile. One is reminded of the story in the life of her holy patron, St. Francis, how, when he heard a Brother to whom begging was an intense mortification, coming up the road to the monastery, singing with his sack upon his back, he went out to meet him and kissed the shoulder where the sack had lain. " Blessed be my Brother," he cried, " who goes forth promptly, quests humbly and comes back merrily ! "

A few weeks after Margaret's Profession, when Mr. G——, a resident in Edinburgh,

was at the Poor Clare Convent in London, one of the nuns told him that they had a young Sister from Edinburgh in the house, and that she would love to see anyone from her own country. She was accordingly fetched, and they had a little conversation. Margaret was very bright and merry, and he thought her looking particularly well. It was therefore a great surprise to him to hear, a few weeks later, that she had gone—an invalid—to the Sanatorium at Warley.

In a letter to Father A——, written about this time, the Mother Abbess told him that Sister Mary Francis had begun to spit blood, and that the doctor had diagnosed tuberculosis of the throat. He had advised that she should be sent out of London, and they had placed her in the Sanatorium and Nursing Home of the Sisters of Charity at Warley. She was bright and cheerful, and full of trust in Our Lord.

But in spite of heroic attempts at cheerfulness, it was a real heartbreak to Sister Francis

Marillac Sanitorium, Warley.

to leave her convent. She was crying all the way to Warley, and could only comfort herself by whispering over and over again: "It is God's Will." It was part of His Holy Providence—and just what she herself would have desired—that her heartbreak was to be the consolation of others. If she had not been an Extern Sister she could not have been taken out of her enclosure. She would have died in the convent, and the account of those wonderful last days would have been lost to the world.

CHAPTER VIII

WARLEY

" Thou mayest look on this heart of thine as on a precious censer from which evermore ascends to God the incense of the prayer of His own most lovely Heart, of its perpetual humble adoration and blissful worship, of its infinite most gladsome love. And when thou bethinkest thee that this is true, and that thus ever abideth and prayeth within thee thy dearest Lord Jesus—' the same yesterday to-day and for ever,' it behoveth thee not to vex thyself overmuch for the distresses that may befall thee, knowing that these disturb not His worship nor His prayer within thy soul; knowing too that He who thus is in thee and who tenderly loveth thee, will do for thee all that thou canst not do, so only that thou put thy whole trust in the love of His most gentle, steadfast Heart—the Heart of the little Babe, the Heart of the Crucified, so helpless and so weak, who is omnipotent God, the Maker and Master of all that is—and thy true Lover, Friend and Spouse! What canst thou fear? Thou art His. He will be thy strength and thy peace."

SOON after Margaret's arrival at Warley her mother and her eldest brother came to see her.

They found her bright and merry, says her sister, and she was delighted to see them. In the following August she wrote to her mother:

"How pleased I am to hear that you had such a nice holiday at Broughty Ferry, it will do you such a lot of good." The rest of the letter consists of family interests and questions; it is only at the end that there is mention of herself. "Our dear Mother Abbess sent the Sisters to see me yesterday, so I am being quite spoilt; it is so good of Mother Abbess to think of her poor, ignorant child in this way and to bestow such love and kindness on me—do pray hard, dear Mother, sisters and brothers, that our dear Lord will reward her great charity a thousandfold." Father A——, she says, has been to see her—may God reward his great charity. "Sister M. R. called to see me on her way to Lourdes; wasn't it kind of her? I am allowed up for a little while some days."

She seems to have had a conviction that she would not get better, and in another letter.

written to her mother a little later, she prepares her gently for the end:

"Now, dear Mother, you must not build up your hopes too high and expect a miracle, for one week I might be very well and the next I might not be well at all, but I am better again." Mother Abbess had "spoilt her again" by permitting the Sisters to come and see her.

In a letter to Sister M. R., a Sister of the Convent of Mercy in Edinburgh, who had visited her on the way to Lourdes, she writes:

"What an unexpected joy to hear from you, I was delighted to receive your letter telling me all about Lourdes, it must be wonderful to see the devotion of so many people. I think you were there at the best time during French National Pilgrimage. . . . On Saturday I received a bottle of Lourdes water and feel sure it has come from you although the

Marillac Sanatorium, showing part of the grounds.

postmark is London. I am very grateful for it, may God reward your great charity. When first I became ill, dear Mother Abbess gave me Lourdes water and the Community made a novena to Our Lady, but to all appearance it is our dear Lord's Holy Will that I should carry the Cross, so I am very happy."

"She suffered very much physically," wrote the Sister Superior of Warley to Father A—— on the death of Sister Mary Francis, "from prostrating weakness, from constant breathlessness and choking in her throat, and from the humiliating necessities caused by her illness. She suffered also from loneliness, from being outside her dear convent and away from her Mother Abbess. She suffered from being transferred from one part of the house to another because her distressing, racking cough disturbed others.[1]

"She suffered, too, from having to wait so long for death. Though she was longing to

[1] She was brought back again, later, to the nun's quarters.

go, she remained always calm and resigned to God's most Holy Will, and she was always smiling. No word or breath of complaint or murmur ever crossed her lips. She was always thanking God for everything and saying how good He was to her, and she so worthless. Holy Communion was her life.

"Her obedience was perfect. I might have been her Abbess—she never seemed to question what I said.

"All who approached her — and priests especially—seemed to be much impressed by her holiness. Bishop ——, from Australia, went in to bless her on the eve of her death and whispered earnestly to her. As we came out of the room I said to him: 'That is a wonderful little soul, my Lord.' 'Yes,' he answered, 'you can see it in her eyes.'

"Several times I wondered where her faults were; I failed to discover any, and I saw her under great trials and sufferings, physical and otherwise. She was indeed a marvel."

" I was impressed, as everyone was, I think, who saw her," writes Father T——, S.J., who was supplying at the parish church at Warley for the few weeks following Sister Francis's arrival at the Sanatorium. " To analyse impressions is not easy, but I think that, in her case, it was surely her childlike innocence that must have been the cause. This manifested itself in a radiant happiness under all circumstances. Owing to her cough, which disturbed others, it was necessary to remove her to another part of the house. I know she felt it keenly, for it meant that she would be isolated from the other Sisters. When I saw her after the change had taken place, although tears were welling from her eyes, yet she was still smiling. Indeed, it seemed impossible for her ever to be gloomy or depressed—a striking instance of the fact that goodness means happiness.

" Another thing that struck me was her devotion and reverence in receiving Our Lord in the Blessed Sacrament. She used to close her eyes and join her hands as an innocent child

who was vividly conscious of His Presence would do. She never complained, though she suffered much from her inability to retain food, and still more from her separation from her religious Sisters in her own convent.

"If she belonged to the slums, she is only another example of the miracles of God's grace, which we priests are privileged to witness in the souls of those who, though materially poor, are yet rich in the things of the spirit."

"She was always suffering, always cheerful," writes another priest who saw a good deal of her. "She never seemed in the least depressed, and edified all around her by her most exemplary patience and resignation. She wanted nothing but to do the Will of God, and I could only marvel how one so young could have attained to such a degree of heroic virtue. . . . It is almost a universal concomitant of the disease from which she suffered to be dissatisfied and hard to please, but Sister Francis never showed the least sign of

impatience. She never asked for any relief, she was perfectly resigned to the Will of God, and during the time I knew her she simply waited with patience the certain summons of death.

" She was certainly a most privileged soul, and must have been most faithful to the call she received from God to dedicate herself to His service. She had the real spirit of her Order, and probably did more by her hidden life than many others have done in a long and active life among men."

The priest who is chaplain in ordinary at the Marillac Sanatorium writes as follows:

" My frequent visits to her always impressed and uplifted me. She was very spiritual but she had a keen sense of humour, and up to the last she thoroughly enjoyed a good joke.

" Her love of God was wonderful. On one occasion she said to me through her tears: ' How nice it is to be able to suffer for His sake ! '

I

"The outcome of her love of God was a corresponding love for souls. 'It is all for souls,' she would exclaim after an extra severe bout of pain. I have been told of her conscientiousness at work while in the convent and how full of life and fun she was withal, and I well remember how delighted she was one day when I took her an apple from the tree she used to attend to in the convent grounds. She loved her convent, and loved to go back to it in spirit, and was ever grateful to God for her vocation."

"She was very spiritual, but up to the last she thoroughly enjoyed a joke." Margaret's sense of humour never left her, even when facing death. One is reminded of her fellow-countryman, the Ven. John Ogilvie, Jesuit and martyr. When he was on his way to the scaffold, a Presbyterian minister, shocked at the apparent levity with which he was laughing with those around him, asked if he were not afraid to be so merry when he was so near his

death. "We have a proverb in Scotland," replied the priest: 'It's past joking when the head's off!'". "Margaret loved Father Ogilvie," says her mother. "She had a book about him, and was always telling us stories out of it. They were kindred spirits."

"One day," says one of the Sisters, "when Sister Francis was still able to be up for a little while with the other invalids, a new nun, by name Sister Clare, was brought in. Sister Francis glanced at her. 'She is the only lady among you,' she said calmly to the others. They were slightly astonished. 'You are all Bernards, or Johns or Columbas,' she explained, laughing."

In the beginning of August, Father A——, S.J., who was in England giving retreats, went, at the request of the Mother Abbess, to see Margaret at Warley. His visit was a great joy to her, for she could pour out her heart to him as she could to no one else. One thing was distressing her. If she did not get better, she said, she would not be allowed to

make her perpetual vows. Father A—— told her that Our Lord would take care of that. "He is always with you," he said.

"Yes," she answered, "He is always with me—like playing with me. And you know, when I took my vows there were lots of people and things, and He asked me whether I liked all that and whether I would not rather be alone with Him. And I only wanted Him. And I never got ill before my vows, but only afterwards, and He showed me how He sent the sickness afterwards, one morning when I coughed and spat blood."

"Have you some nice name for Him?" he asked.

"Sweet Jesus."

"Does He ever answer?"

"Yes. 'My Love.'"

"Did you ever see Him?"

"Yes. Very sad."

"Did you hear Him with your ears?"

"No. Just within me here."

"Was it with your eyes you saw Him?"

" No."

" Did you feel Him? "

" No," with a most emphatic shake of the head.

" That is right," said he, " for those things are very dangerous."

He asked her many other questions, for he wanted to make sure that she had no delusions. She was sitting up in bed facing the window, with the light full on her face. She was looking well, the simplicity of her soul shining in her clear eyes—" those startlingly clear, grey, candid eyes," as someone called them. Two things were troubling her. Our Lord, she said, had taken away the Cross from her, and she wanted to suffer for Him. She was also anxious about obedience. She wanted to say her Office, as the holy rule of her Order enjoined, but Our Lord was so constantly with her that she could not. On this point He reassured her, telling her that when Our Lord was holding her soul in contemplation it meant that He did not require it. This

filled her with joy.   It was a load off her mind.

"Her thirst for suffering was intense," says Father A——.   "I had to stop her mortifications in Edinburgh."   He wrote in his letter of recommendation of Margaret to her Mother Abbess, that she was inclined to excessive mortifications, but that he foresaw no difficulty, as she was perfectly docile.

Father A—— asked her what books she read, and she showed him the *Imitation of Christ* and the New Testament.   She liked best, she said, the seventh and eighth chapters of the Second Book of the Imitation —"Of the Love of Jesus above All Things" and "Of Familiar Friendship with Jesus"— and the fifth chapter of the Third Book—"Of the Wonderful Effects of Divine Love."

He then explained to her—from the Gospel of St. John and the Epistles of St. Paul—the wonderful doctrine of the Mystical Body of Christ, and how, through union with Him, as His members, every smallest detail of life

acquires an infinite value. She asked him to show her the various passages, so that she could go over them herself, and he did so, telling her that she had a great part to play for Christ, and quoting to her St. Paul's words: " I rejoice therefore in my sufferings." (Col. I, 24.)

He asked if she would like to go to confession, and she said she would. She made a general confession of her whole innocent life, during which she had not committed one single deliberate venial sin. He warned her not to make too much of the intimate favours she was receiving from her Lord. They did not mean greater holiness, he said, and He could stop them at any moment. He would, in all probability, hide Himself for a time, but she must comfort herself in the thought that she was doing His most Holy Will.

There was no difficulty there, he found; she was not inclined that way; there was no trace in her of pride or of self-consciousness. He became more convinced than ever that these

intimacies with her Divine Spouse were not new to her; she showed too clearly that she had been long accustomed to converse with Him in the simplicity of her heart. He felt some anxiety lest, as her illness advanced and the fatigue, the suffering and the loneliness increased, she might have to pass through some such ordeal as was experienced by St. John Berchmans or the Little Flower. Apparently, however, judging from what the Sisters of Charity at Warley say of her last days, she did not do so.

On his way back to Scotland, when the August and September retreats were over, Father A—— came to see Margaret again. What struck him most at this second visit was the intense yearning of her soul for her Divine Spouse—" a veritable purgatory—an unquenchable thirst of soul which baffles description. It seemed as if her whole soul was poured out in the whisper : ' I want to see Him, Father.' ' As the hart panteth after the fountains of water, so did her soul pant after

Him.' ' I adjure you if you find my Beloved, that you tell Him that I am sick of love.' "

He had no longer any misgivings. There was no fear of any struggle in her soul—" I live, yet not I, but Christ liveth in me."

" Our Lord always makes Himself present with you? " he asked.

" He is always with me."

" And you let Him do just what He pleases? "

" Yes."

" You will not forget that your holiness consists in doing just what you are told, for love of Him? "

" No, Father."

" Does anyone else speak to you? "

" Our Lady."

" What do you call her? "

" Mother."

" Is it often? "

" When He hides Himself, she comes to comfort me."

" Anyone else? "

" St. Joseph, once.   I was very surprised, because I have no special devotion to him.   It was when my cough was very bad in the night."

" Anyone else? "

" My Angel Guardian helps me to keep awake in the morning and prepare myself for Holy Communion when I have been very bad at night."

" Was it the same," she asked him, " if she could only hear the bells of the Mass from her room, without being actually present? "

He told her that every Mass was said in the name of, and for all Catholics who wished to join themselves to it, and that she could unite herself to all the Masses that were being said in the whole world.   This delighted her.

She must not be afraid, he said, if Our Lord were to hide Himself from her for a little while.   He was there, all the same, in the depths of her soul.

She was ready to leave all that—like every-

thing else—to Him, and told him that she was perfectly happy.

"What struck me most about Sister Mary Francis," writes a Sister of Charity[1] who nursed her during nine months at Warley, " was the heroic patience in her great sufferings. She had tuberculosis of the lungs and throat, and at times the cough was so troublesome that she could not retain any food. She was told that she must try to do so, and she was so perfectly obedient in even the smallest things that she would try her utmost to do it.

"Another thing that impressed me very much was her great spirit of recollection. She seemed to live always in the Presence of God, yet she never made a show of holiness. Indeed, it was her great reserve that impressed me the most, together with her humility and charity. Never once did I hear her say an uncharitable word, and she was so grateful for even the smallest services.

[1] Sister C—— is now in Ireland.

"She had always the same sweet, heavenly smile, and never, even in her greatest sufferings, forgot her little word of thanks: 'May God reward you, Sister!' 'Oh, how good God is to me!' she would often say. As a rule patients suffering from her complaint are exacting and hard to please; Sister Francis was an exception, she seemed to have no likes or dislikes. She kept her little secrets well, and did her mortification very quietly.

"She would never ask for anything. One day I brought her some grapes and she looked very pleased. 'Oh, Sister,' she said, 'isn't God good to me? He sends me everything I wish for. Only yesterday I was longing for some grapes, and now here they are.'

"She never murmured or complained, even on the days when she suffered the most. Once, when she had had a bad attack of pain in her side, she said to me in the evening: 'Oh, Sister, this has been a glorious day.'

"'Why?' I asked.

"'A day of great suffering,' she said, with

her sweet smile. 'If I could only gain one soul for Jesus, it would be worth it all.' She seemed to offer all her sufferings for the salvation of souls.

" She had a great love for her holy vocation, and was most faithful in following, as far as she could, all the rules and customs of her religious life. She would resist any little attempt to make her more comfortable, if she thought it was not in the spirit of her Order. Yet she was perfectly obedient, and one had only to say: 'This is a hospital, Sister, and there are to be no mortifications here,' for her to yield at once, and let us do all we wanted. I often felt that it was a great humiliation to her.

" We had such a high opinion of her holiness that visitors who came to Marillac House were nearly always brought in to see her. One of the characteristics of her illness is the deceptive appearance of health. I often noticed that sometimes, when she was feeling very tired, visitors would come in, and not

understanding how ill she was, would say to her : ' Oh, you are quite well, Sister, there can be nothing the matter with you.' I often thought it must have cost her pain, but she never mentioned it.

"She loved St. Francis, St. Clare and St. Colette, and she used to tell me lovely little stories about them. When she heard that the Franciscan Fathers had made a Foundation in Edinburgh, she was full of joy. She could talk of nothing else all that day. ' Is it not grand?' she would exclaim again and again, ' to think that they are back again, after all those years; how much good they will be able to do for souls!'"

Her mother, with John, the eldest son, went to visit Margaret at Marillac House in the June of 1925, a few months after she went there. "She was quite cheerful and merry," says her sister, ' but when Mother and I and John went again in October, she was so weak that we could hardly catch her words. But

she was still smiling. She spoke of all the kindness she had received from her Mother Abbess and the Sisters at Warley. She wanted to have Mother to herself, and suggested that John and I should go for a walk in the grounds."

They stayed at Marillac House for a few days. "Sister Francis was overjoyed to have them," says Sister C——, "though she was very tired. She was very anxious that her sister L—— should devote herself very lovingly to her mother. The day before they left for home, she gave them all a little souvenir which had been sent her by Mother Abbess. The parting was most edifying. Though her poor mother was heartbroken, she kept perfectly calm while she was with Sister Mary Francis, but once out of her sight, she broke down completely. 'Well,' she said, 'I have given her to God long since, now He can take her. May His Holy Will be done.'

" She was always delighted when the Sisters from her Convent came to see her. They

brought her all the Community news, which pleased her, and told her about Mother Abbess, whom she loved very much. Once an apple was brought her from the little tree of which she had had charge. It was its first fruit, and there was great joy that day. The apple was cooked for her, and she had great delight in it, for it was from her dear convent home.

"All who saw her were much impressed, especially priests. 'Mind that little nun, Sister, she is a saint,' said one who saw her for the first time, as he came out of the room. She seems to have made a great impression on him, for he wrote afterwards to ask for her prayers. He now treasures a bit of her habit.

"She seemed to be just such another as the Little Flower; Jesus was her all. How she loved to see the Holy Name, which she had opposite her bed, decorated with flowers!

"One day, when she was trying to sleep, she was suddenly seized with a fit of coughing and a wasp got down her throat and stung her. For a moment she was really frightened, and

I could not help wondering why one who had already so much to suffer, should have this extra pain. To my surprise she said : ' Only another little splinter of the Cross.' She must have suffered from it for days.

" Though she had no fear of death, she would often ask to have the prayers of the Church said, lest she might die during the night. She answered them all, and was then quite happy. She must have been very lonely ' Ah, Sister, why should I look for human consolation?' Then she would thank me so sweetly for any little word or act.

" Once I said to her : ' Your life as a Poor Clare must be a hard one. Were you ever hungry?' 'Yes,' she answered, 'that was a real joy!'

" I could not see a fault in her, and I asked her to look after me when she got to heaven. ' Yes, Sister,' was her answer, ' I never, never will forget you,' and I feel, for many reasons, that she is faithfully keeping her promise."

K

" I saw the little Poor Clare Colettine only three or four times," wrote Father K——, S.J., to Father A——, " but during that short time I realized what a humble, saintly soul she was—always smiling, in spite of her suffering and forced inactivity. Like her Patron, St. Francis, she was fond of birds that cheered up her last moments at Warley. Ma Sœur Burd had a canary which she placed beside the bed of this humble violet, and its antics and sweet notes were a source of happy, childlike joy to her.

" She was so genuinely grateful, too, for all and everything that was done for her. When I visited her once, about three months before her death, she was lying at full length on a wheeled chair. I asked her about her little friend, the canary, which used to be by her bed, and whether I should get it for her. She seemed so pleased and happy when I brought it; it raised her mind to her heavenly Father, Who feeds and cares for all His creatures. I am glad of this opportunity of giving you this

last message of gratitude to you from her for all your kindness to her. Even at that last visit, weak and exhausted, she was still smiling, still thoughtful of others, still grateful—a humble little violet."

CHAPTER IX

DEATH

" Blessed art thou, O Sister Death, who art to me the gate of Life."—St. Francis of Assisi.

" Thus the dove-soul returns to the Ark of God, not only white and pure as it went forth when He created it, but with the olive branch of reward and peace obtained by the conquest of itself."—St. John of the Cross.

It was obvious to all that the end could not be far off. " I have sent on your letter to Sister M. Francis," wrote the Mother Abbess to Mrs. Sinclair, shortly before Margaret's death; " she is wonderful, and how she must be longing to go to heaven. It is nice to know that she only wants God's Will. . . .

" I sent two Sisters down to see her yesterday. Sister M. Francis is not able to write now; she is very, very weak, and is unable to

talk much. She is quite happy and quite resigned to God's Holy Will. . . .

" She is lucky to be winning her crown so early in her religious life, but she has been generous with Our Lord, so she is ready to answer His Call. I know it will be a great consolation to you to know that your child is our dear Lord's own little spouse, and a very favoured one too. She must do great things for you and for us when she gets to heaven."

She had no fear of death, says Sister C——, and talked about it as she would have done of her Profession day. " Her one anxiety was to have her holy habit on when she was dying, and a copy of her holy vows, her crucifix and the blessed candle in her hand. Indeed, she always had in her hand, or close beside it, the copy of her vows and the little crucifix that she kept attached by a string to her wrist.

" She would talk about the Requiem Mass, and when suffering **very** much, she loved to

speak of the joys to come. Her one great
desire was for Holy Communion. On one
occasion, when she had a very bad turn, we
really thought she was dying. She was so ill
and exhausted that the chaplain came to give
her Holy Viaticum. I stayed beside her bed
for some time afterwards, and I shall never
forget the beautiful expression of her face. I
could not take my eyes off her; it was a
heavenly look, and she was smiling, as if at
some heavenly vision. After a little while I
said to her: 'Sister Mary Francis, are you
smiling at the angels?' 'Perhaps,' she
answered, in her calm, reserved way. Then
I said: 'Did you ever see Our Blessed Lady?'
'Yes, Sister,' she answered. Whether she saw
her then or not, I don't know. She kept her
secrets well and made no show of her piety,
but one felt that one was in the presence of a
truly holy soul. She was so refined in every
way, it was hardly possible to believe that she
had been born and brought up in a slum."

"I saw her at Marillac House," writes a

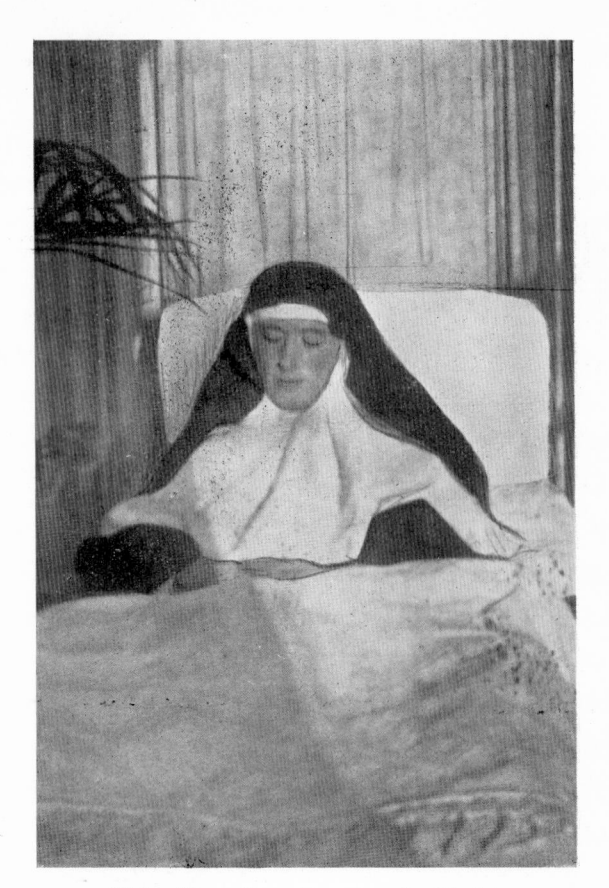

Sister Mary Francis on her deathbed.
(From a Photograph taken a few hours before she died.)

priest, "in August, 1925. I had just been ordained priest and went to see my aunt, a Sister of Charity, who was ill with consumption there. She was most insistent on my seeing ' the little Poor Clare.' I went to Sister Mary Francis and gave her my new blessing and spoke to her. She was the centre of attraction in the house. I saw her again the next day. She had just had a severe fit of vomiting, the nursing Sister told me, but she was wonderfully cheerful, smiling most beautifully all the time. I left on the 8th, and did not see her again, though I thought much about her. I was not a bit surprised, but extremely gratified, to hear later of her great sanctity."

A Sister who only knew Margaret during the last three weeks of her life and was her night nurse during that period, writes :

" She was suffering much, but every little thing I did for her was greeted with the sweetest smile and her favourite phrase : ' May God reward you, Sister ! ' All through the

night she coughed incessantly; I sometimes thought she would choke. With all this there was never a single word of complaint. Sometimes she would doze for a little while. Then she would open her eyes, looking so peaceful and radiant, and offer up her favourite ejaculation: 'JESUS.' Then, from two o'clock in the morning she would prepare for Holy Communion, which was her one desire and her only happiness. Her attitude during those long nights of suffering is more than I can express.

"Each night she was getting weaker, with very bad attacks of breathlessness, but with always the same sweet smiling face, and kissing her crucifix till the hour of her death. Such a beautiful death I have never witnessed. The whole night through she was saying little prayers, such as: 'Jesus, forgive me all my faults'; 'Jesus, Mary, Joseph, I give you my heart and my soul,' and kissing her crucifix, a most happy expression on her face.

"At about three she became weaker, but was

still conscious, saying the same little prayers
with such fervour. She was conscious to the
end. Her last prayer was: 'Jesus, Mary,
Joseph, I give you my heart and my soul.'
That last prayer made such an impression
on me; it was said with such fervour and
confidence that one felt that she was
already in the arms of Jesus, Mary and
Joseph.

" It was the 24th of November, and Sister
Mary Francis was twenty-five years old."

In a letter to her mother they wrote:

" She was conscious to the last and edified
all around her. Last night her body was
taken to her convent. We followed her down
to the gate—two priests in front, and the little
altar boy with processional crucifix. We
walked behind with lighted candles."

" She was laid out in the room where
she died," says Sister C——. " She looked
heavenly, just as if she were peacefully sleep-
ing. She never lost that angelic smile, even

in death. That evening she was taken by hearse to the convent at Notting Hill, leaving Warley at half-past five. It was very impressive to see the solemn little procession winding its way down the avenue. The chaplain and some other priests followed the hearse, chanting prayers, then came nuns and Sisters, their lighted candles shining out in the dark November evening. At her own convent the coffin was met by her own community, also with lighted candles, and carried to the chapel.

" She was buried in Kensal Green cemetery. The coffin was covered with the most beautiful white flowers, some of them the gift of the little bridesmaids of her Profession-day. It was a small funeral; the chaplain, a few Poor Clare Sisters, two Sisters of Charity, and two Little Sisters of the Poor were all the company attending it. The cemetery looked lonely and aloof, but yet so beautiful under its white veil of snow. We all wept with sorrow for our loss, and with joy to think that her sufferings

Sister Mary Francis Sinclair's Grave in Kensal Green
Cemetery.

at last were over and that she had gone to her Jesus Whom she had loved so much."

" I shall always consider it my greatest privilege in this world," says Sister C——, " to have been with her during her illness and at the hour of her holy death."

" She had a most beautiful death and was conscious to the very end," wrote another, " and she was delighted to be going to the God she had loved so much and served so faithfully. She is one of the most beautiful souls I ever met, and it was a privilege to have to do anything for her. I feel more disposed to pray to her than for her."

" Our dear little child has at last gone to her reward," wrote the Mother Abbess to her mother, " and how happy she must be after her life of love and union with her Beloved. One cannot think of her anywhere but in heaven."

" I have just been seeing your darling little child," she wrote later, " and she looks lovely, with a sweet smile on her face and so peaceful

and calm. I am sending you the little crucifix she had always in her hand, with the little red string on it just as she had it. I think it is the biggest treasure she had. I am going to get a nice wreath of flowers from you with the pound you gave me.

"She looks so lovely, and the coffin is still open. I am sure Sister Mary Francis will do much for us from heaven. One cannot but feel very happy about her—and I am sure you do." The Mother Abbess had bought a wreath of roses, lilies, heather and violets to represent her family, who were unable to be there. She sent two of the violets in her letter. "The sun is shining as I write, after a hard frost," she wrote again, "and I think of what must be the ' brightness of God ' which has shone on that pure soul, fresh from the consecration of her vows to Him, and after the sufferings which He had allowed her as a mark of His special love for her."

"Everyone loved her in the convent here," wrote one of Margaret's Sisters in religion to

her mother, " and you must have seen the love your dear child inspired at Warley, where everything possible was done for her. We feel that the light of God's most beautiful Home was dawning upon her just as the dawn of the day would be breaking." (She died in the early hours of the morning.)

" It is a great consolation to me to feel that our dear Lord bestowed so many of His choicest graces on Sister Mary Francis," wrote her Mother Abbess to Father A——. " I am sure she will do great things from heaven for us all."

" The next time I saw her," writes the friend who was present at Margaret's Profession, " she was in her coffin. I have seen many dead people, but never have I seen a face so beautiful in death. She was in no way changed, and it is impossible to describe her expression. Sister K——, who stood with me beside her, said that one could never imagine that soul going to purgatory, even for a moment."

"It was wonderful," says Sister C——. "Just before burial, they opened up the coffin and crowned the pale brow with a wreath of laurels—the sign of victory."

And down the centuries come the undying words of one who himself had striven and had won the crown of life: "So run that you may obtain. . . . Everyone that striveth for the mastery refraineth himself from all things: and they indeed that they may receive a corruptible crown, but we an incorruptible one. I therefore so run—not as at an uncertainty." . . .

On the 21st of December, all the necessary sanctions having been obtained by the Scottish National Margaret Sinclair Committee, the body of St. Mary Francis of the Five Wounds was exhumed from the grave in Kensal Green Cemetery, and brought to Edinburgh, to be re-interred the next day in the Mount Vernon Cemetery at Liberton.

Formula of Vows found in the coffin of Sister Mary Francis.

APPENDIX

EXTRACT from a letter written to the author by Father X, a Redemptorist, who was replacing the parish priest when Margaret went to Rosewell for her holiday:

"I went to Penicuik on August 3rd, a Saturday, and stayed till the following Saturday, August 10th, on which day I left for London in order to give a retreat to the Daughters of the Cross at Great Yarmouth, commencing on the Monday following. I mention these apparently irrelevant details for the purpose of showing you that I have an unusually retentive memory for facts. In spite, however, of my good memory, I had completely forgotten the Rosewell holiday until it was evoked by the reading of Margaret Sinclair's life.

" During my supply, I said Mass on the Sunday, August 4th, both at Penicuik and Rosewell, Penicuik being then the parish church, Rosewell the succursal school and chapel. On the weekdays, Monday to Friday, I said Mass at Penicuik. On Saturday I said Mass at Rosewell.

" From the beginning of my stay I had noticed two girls, obviously sisters, attending church very regularly, both at Penicuik and Rosewell. I took more notice of them from the fact that the distance between the two places was about five miles, as far as I remember, and the other fact that the weather all that week was extremely wet and unseasonable. One morning it rained so heavily that I made sure they would not come, and began Mass (at Penicuik) before the time announced. Margaret came : about Bella I am not sure. In fact, I think Bella missed that morning.

" As I have said, I noticed the girls at every service, or nearly every service. I am not ready to affirm that they went to Mass at both

places on the Sunday, but I incline to opine that they did, as also to Benediction at both places. Be this as it may, they made such an impression on me by their quiet and modest piety and a certain indefinable something, that, acting on a sudden impulse, I determined to speak to them, after Mass, on the last morning.

"As a priest and Redemptorist I am very reserved with women, especially young ladies. Never before had I sought the acquaintance of pious maidens, nor have I sought it since. Again I am very averse to giving gratuitous advice. Least of all am I disposed to bestow quasi-patriarchal blessings on maidenly heads. Yet I did all this, acting upon a sudden inspiration.

" Bella's account of the interview is substantially correct, but I should like to subjoin my own.

" I began by apologizing for having sent for them. They were very shy and timid, afraid, as I suppose, of my six feet and a quarter. I

L

asked them their surname, and, being rather deaf, did not catch it at first. 'Sinclair,' said Bella, distinctly. Then I asked their Christian names. 'Margaret,' said the one, 'Bella,' the other. (I recognize them both from the photographs in your book.) And their place of origin. 'Edinburgh,' said Bella. I then said how edified I had been by their regular attendance at Mass and by their daily Communion, that they were very good girls, but that it was not enough to have begun, that they must continue. Unconsciously, I laid my hands on their shoulders, and spoke gravely about the love of God and His service, and repeated what I said, speaking, as it were, soul to soul, and giving them my best blessing. Finally, I again apologized for calling them into the sacristy, and after receiving their answer, dismissed them, being very much astonished at my conduct immediately afterwards—astonished and confused.

"I cannot describe to you precisely the impression they made upon me. I could not

analyse it then, I cannot now. All I can say is : it was an 'indefinable something' which made them seem different from other girls. Especially Margaret. To this day I can see the look in her clear and open eyes as I spoke to her and her sister, a look which said : ' Yes, I will do all I can to love God and make Him loved.'

" In outward appearance the two girls were very refined. I thought they were teachers, or boarders at a convent, if I thought anything. They were well dressed, both alike, in dark blue coats. But it was their interior radiance which shone out through their exterior features that made an impression which still lasts."